out of print Ba t 50

Reminiscences of Reading

An Octogenarian

Edited by
Daphne Phillips

COUNTRYSIDE BOOKS
NEWBURY, BERKSHIRE

First Published 1889

This edition published by
Countryside Books 1985

COUNTRYSIDE BOOKS
3 Catherine Road
Newbury, Berkshire

ISBN 0 905392 39 6

Designed by Mon Mohan/Jo Angell

Produced through MRM (Print Consultants) Ltd., Reading, Berks.
Printed in England by J.W. Arrowsmith Ltd., Bristol

Contents

William Silver Darter, 1803-97

Introduction

Reminiscences of Reading, by An Octogenarian, first appeared as a series of articles in the Reading Observer newspaper 1884-88, and were published in book form in the following year. The author was William Silver Darter, a well-loved and respected senior citizen and raconteur who had served the town for 45 years as councillor, Mayor (1850-52), alderman and magistrate.

By trade he had been a plumber, painter and glazier; a line of business which brought him into contact with a great many interesting people and gave him an intimate knowledge of public and private buildings. This knowledge was the source of many of his favourite reminiscences. On one occasion, at a political dinner party at Rose Hill House in Caversham, he startled his host and the distinguished guests around the table by remarking that he knew the house well, for in that very room he had once made a lead coffin for a former owner.

His trade had also given him a special knowledge of the town's essential services. He could talk informatively yet entertainingly about the shortcomings of the early water supply, the introduction of gas lighting, and his own contribution to the great public health enquiry of 1847. A lifelong Liberal, he strove throughout his years on the council to improve the town's amenities and to better living conditions for the poor. In the 1830s, before the Borough Police Force was established, he served as a part-time constable for the parish of St. Giles; and many years later, when he was chief magistrate, he exerted himself to improve the efficiency of the police.

He was born in London Street, Reading, in a house near the Crown Inn, on 3 December 1803 and christened William Silver at St Giles in the following January. His father, a carpenter who had formerly held some minor government office, had married Mary, widow of Joshua Silver of Caversham, by whom she had two daughters. In 1805 a younger brother, George, was born but less than two years later Mary died at the age of 37.

Very little is known about William's home life but it is evident in his reminiscences that he enjoyed a gread deal of freedom out of doors. He was an active, enterprising, adventurous youth, blessed with wide-ranging interests. He explored the streets and courts and alleyways of his home town, got to know the inhabitants and delved a little into the history of the old buildings. A lover of music, he sang in the church choir and performed very creditably on the flute at public concerts. A keen swimmer, he knew all the local bathing places well, and in later years rescued several drowning people from the river. He attended the rowdy political meetings of those days and listened to speeches in inn yards. He witnessed the rough, often cruel, sports which were then so popular and roundly condemned the brutalities of bull-baiting and prize fighting.

Had he been born a few years earlier he would certainly have enlisted to fight Napoleon. As it was, the years of his childhood were coloured by the hardships and excitements of the wars against the French; and throughout his life recollections of the men who marched away, and the stories told by those who returned from the battlefields, never failed to stir him. As soon as he was old enough he joined the Woodley Troop of the Berkshire Yeomanry commanded by Captain Montague, although the war had been over for six years, and at least twice he travelled to Belgium to visit the field of Waterloo.

At the age of 21 he set up in business at 21 London Street and, a year or two later, married Maria Jenkins of Bristol. In 1827 the couple moved to a better house at 26 London Street. Sadly, of their seven children, three died in infancy and were buried in St. Giles' new churchyard with William's father, who had died on Christmas Day 1825. In his work, however, he prospered and within a few years built up a large and lucrative business. One story illustrating his shrewdness and foresight tells how, while travelling to London during a terrific thunderstorm, he anticipated that there would be a great number of broken windows and conservatories to be repaired, and so bought up all the glass he could in London and had it forwarded immediately to Reading.

It was fortunate for him, and for us his readers, that Darter lived for so many years in London Street, in those days the liveliest, busiest, most handsome thoroughfare in Reading, and inhabited by a wonderful variety of trades and professional men. There he was able to watch stage coaches and wagons passing up and down, private carriages drawing up outside George Lovejoy's famous bookshop, soldiers marching and bands playing, recruiting officers at work in the local inns, ragged prisoners of war being brought into the town, and on special occasions, public dinners for the poor in the open air. In 1827 he was proud to give up his first floor drawing room with its three balconies to Captain Montague and his family, to enable them to watch the magnificent procession in honour of Charles Fyshe Palmer, Reading's popular M.P.

By 1839 Darter was wealthy enough to move to a new house, called Swiss Villa, in Kings Road, and a few years later to a larger new house called Sutherlands at Whitley. There, in 1855, his wife died. In 1865 Darter retired from business, but not from public life in which he continued up to the age of 90. About 1877 he moved into a third new house which he had built on the corner of Christchurch and Vicarage Roads. It was called Somerleaze; and there he died on 13 April 1897, aged 93.

When he was a little over 80 he was approached by the Liberal *Reading Observer* with a proposal to publish his recollections of Reading in the early part of the 19th century. Hence the reminiscences that follow recall the coaching age rather than the age of the railway and the industrial expansion of the town.

Milk below!

AN OLD READING CHARACTER.

'Milk Below' - a street milk vendor of the early ninteenth century.

— 1 —
Early Memories

As far back as 1809, I was at school in Portland Place, the master being a Mr. Jameson, late writing master at Dr. Valpy's Grammar School, the assistant-master being a Mr. Warwick, who assited me in my first effort at letter writing. The school would have been a success but for the cruel thrashing some of the boys received at the hands of the Head Master. One pupil from Newbury, of the name of Twitchen, being a strong fellow, resisted, and as the master could not manage him without assistance, he sent to the Crown Hotel for a post boy to help him, and Twitchen was then sent home in a post chaise. This affair brought the school into bad repute, and it soon ceased to exist. During my residence at this school there were no houses in Albion Place; therefore, there was an uninterrupted view of the old goal. One morning, in 1811, I was placed in a chair at a front window, and saw a young man executed; he was only 19 years of age. At this period there were no houses beyond Portland Place until you came to the Marquis of Granby Inn, the whole south side of the London Road being agricultural fields with hedge rows and large trees forming the south boundary to the said road, with a footpath inside the field going to the Granby and another in the direction of the Whiteknights Lake. On the north side of the London Road there was merely a thatched cottage called the Half-Way House, a small house in Watlington Lane (now street) and Collins' Farm, which stood where St. John's Church is erected. All the land in question was agricultural and was called Garrard's Farm. There was only one path which ran from the Granby down to Silly Bridge. The land upon which Huntley and Palmers' works, the gas works, &c., now stand, was meadows. Boult's Wharf, now called South Street, the Grove, Queen's Crescent, &c., consisted of two deep gravel pits with a

11

lane running from the London Road (now called Sidmouth Street) dividing the two pits and terminating in Star Lane, or rather Messrs. Blandy and Palmers' Wharf, now Messer and Co's. The King's Road was made in 1832-3. The first sale of the land in plots took place in 1833, the second in 1835, and the vendors were the Commissioners of Woods and Forests. The Queen's Road was formed by the Corporation of Reading about the same period as the King's Road. At this time Sir. Wm. Scott (Dr. Johnson's executor), afterwards created Lord Stowel, lived at Earley House, late the residence of Mr. Charles Stephens.

Prior to this, Reading Races, more commonly called Bulmershe Heath Races, were held there up to and including the year 1815, when they ceased. The course was about three miles, and within my memory the races were well supported. The Captain of our Troop of Yeomanry (Captain Montagu) used to invite Fuller Craven and others of his old comrades when he himself was in the Regulars, and drove four in hand to the races, usually accompanied by a keyed bugle player seated in the rear.

Bulmershe Heath was enclosed, I think, as early as 1816. I myself was in the Yeomanry in 1821, and at that time we assembled there, the enclosure occurring some years previously. Many cottagers used to cut the heather turf on the common, which they dried in summer, and it served them for fire and to heat their ovens. An old servant of ours married and occupied one of the small houses on the edge of the heath, in which two or three generations of the family had lived, and who had always been accustomed to rear geese and poultry on the common, but when the late Mr. Wheble's father enclosed the heath, all these privileges were swept away.

To revert again to Sidmouth Street, it may interest some to know that the Quakers' burying-ground was in this street at the north-west angle of the wall which encloses the garden to the first house in Albion Place. There was a house adjoining, in which lived the parents of the present Mr. Smith, builder, of Watlington Street. The whole of this was removed to the present Friends' burying-ground in or about the year 1829. On looking at the underpinning of the late Mr. G. May's wall, on the west side of the road, it will be seen that the road and burying-ground stood many feet higher than the site is now.

It will soon be forgotten that the Bluecoat School was originally in the London Road, the building being afterwards a model lodging-house, and now used for St. Giles' Boys' and Girls' Schools. I remember Mr. May, Master of the Bluecoat School, having died in the early part of this century, and being a Mason and much respected; he was buried in St. Giles' old churchyard with Masonic honours. As I am referring to St. Giles' parish, I will add that in 1811 Mr. George Palmer's house did not exist, and that an Inn named the Row Barge stood where now stands the Royal Berkshire Hotel. Mr. Patey was the landlord and cultivated the gardens. A son of his was a Dragoon, and fought in every battle in the Peninsula, including Corunna and Waterloo. He died in Reading a few years since at the age of 90. Another son assisted his father, and as the garden was frequently robbed, he placed a man-trap in it, and erected a notice board to warn people of his having done so, but, unfortunately, his son inadvertently stepped on the spring and was shot in the leg and became lame for life.

Watlington House, now Kendrick School, was, prior to 1820, an establishment for young ladies, under the management of Mrs. Littleworth, afterwards Mrs. Stevens; and from about 1820 to a recent period it became the residence of the late Capt. Purvis, who, I think from the year 1816, was Adjutant in the Berkshire Militia, and one of the Magistrates for Reading. I may add also that the gallant Captain fought at the battle of Corunna as an officer in the 4th Foot.

Kendrick Hill was, in my early days, merely a foot-path of some seven or eight feet wide, with a hedge on each side, and was called Doll's Walk. It was on the west side of the road, and digressed a little to the east a short distance above High Grove, terminating at the Shinfield Road, commencing again just opposite where Christ Church stands, and continuing straight to Whitley Wood, by which the public had a charming walk in the summer, and they had the opportunity of extending it either to the left into the Shinfield Road, or to the right into the Basingstoke Road. I am anxious to record this because I see that an attempt has been made to stop this path. A similar attempt was made some 40 years since, but as soon as public attention was drawn to it, the young men of the town swept the obstruction away, and it is only recently that these attempts to interfere with public rights have been repeated.

13

The house called The Acacias, now the property of the junior Member for Reading, was erected by Mr. Law, a coal and salt merchant, of Bridge Street, who was also member of the old Corporation; his new house was ironically called Salt Box Hall. Just beyond this house, N.W. corner of Red Lane, and not long before the erection of the Berkshire Hospital, stood an extensive range of stables, occupied by the horses used in the Bath and Bristol coaches, belonging to Mr. Lovegrove, and which suddenly took fire at night and were quickly burnt down, 36 valuable animals being destroyed. I myself witnessed the scene, but so rapidly was the place consumed that neither I nor any others could render assistance. It was most distressing to hear the cries of the perishing horses, and so also was that of seeing four horse coaches arrive, and stop to change at these stables, but finding no fresh teams to relieve them, the poor fatigued creatures were given a little hay and water and driven, I believe, on to Woolhampton (another ten miles).

As I have mentioned the Hospital I will allude to the fact that the principal promoter of its erection was a Mr. Oliver, a Roman Catholic gentleman, who for a long time agitated the question, not only by letters in the newspapers, but by walking through the county and personally soliciting aid for the erection of it from county gentlemen and others, until by continued perseverance he had accomplished this self-imposed task. One distressing fact I have to add, viz., that not very long after this noble and beneficent work was carried out, Mr. Oliver, in crossing the London Road, was run over and so injured that it became necessary to remove him to the hospital, where he died, leaving two daughters totally unprovided for. I only knew one of them myself; she was well educated but in feeble health. The last time I heard of her, she had become an inmate of a workhouse in London. As this accident to poor Mr. Oliver was occasioned by, it was asserted, the careless driving of a servant of one of the largest and most prosperous firms in Reading, I hope if this should meet the eye of one of its members, and if it is not too late, some provision for this unfortunate lady might be made to rescue her from her present humiliating position. I understand from the late Mr. Lovejoy that the father had been managing clerk to a London Bank from which he had retired with a pension for life. This pension ceased at his death.

Whitenights was always a great attraction for the inhabitants of

Reading, particularly during the early part of the century, when it was occupied by the then Marquis of Blandford, afterwards Duke of Marlborough, who, if a man of many faults, was also one of excellent taste and accomplishments. He it was who formed and planted the Wilderness, built the Rustic Bridge and Grottos, supported a private band and admitted the public (subject to certain regulations). I was told an anecdote in reference to the Duke's, or rather Marquis' skill as a musician. He was not only a composer but could arrange for a military band, and it happened that he had composed and arranged a piece with a difficult bass solo; his performers did not execute this solo to please him, and after the practice he was privately informed that a player of the 'serpent' had recently obtained his discharge from the Berkshire Militia Band, which was at the time stationed in Ireland; he was very soon sent for and introduced to the Marquis, who invited him to bring his instrument. The new composition was introduced, and to his astonishment the stranger played if off at sight so splendidly that it made another thing of his overture. The Marquis was so excited and so delighted at the result that he was anxious to praise his band, and the serpent player in particular; but, unfortunately, he had an impediment in his speech, and although he made several attempts, he could not utter a word for a long time. In his efforts to speak he became very red in the face, walked away for a time, and on returning said, 'Middleton, how did you get your discharge?' 'Why, your Grace, I lost an eye.' 'Lost an eye, have you, then by G. you play better with one eye than any fellow I ever heard with two.'

The Marquis bought the adjoining land called Redlands, and planted a belt of trees all round the combined estates, and by leaving an avenue he had a private drive of nearly three miles. People were permitted to skate over the lakes, and the general public enjoyed an uninterrupted walk through the park with their children riding in chaises similar to our modern perambulators. I mention this fact with a desire of calling attention to the attempt now made to exclude this vehicle and thus deprive the working class of a much esteemed right; the thin end of the wedge has already been applied by the placing of a notice board at the entrance lodge, which seems to give authority to the lodge keeper to prevent this traffic. It is doubtful, however, if Lady Goldsmid, who, I believe, has the reversion of the estate, has any knowledge of the matter. As to the right to use the road through the park as a bridle way, I myself have ridden through it without being at all interfered with for more than 30 years prior to the estate being cut up for villas. In confirmation of this statement I may refer to the late Mr. William Blandy, a gentleman who was unfortunately drowned in the winter of 1816. He was fond of horse-back exercise and frequently rode through Whiteknight's Park, but on one occasion, on attempting to do so, he found the gates fastened. He applied to the lodge-keeper to open them, but the keeper refused, stating that he had orders to keep them closed. Mr. Blandy replied, 'If they are not immediately opened I will bring a man with a sledge hammer and force the gates.' This had the desired effect; the gates were opened, and I never heard of any attempt to prevent people riding in the park until recent years.

At this time, and for many years afterwards, there were serious conflicts between Dr. Valpy's pupils and the town boys as to the right of playing on the Forbury green near the Doctor's residence, and which formed the play-ground for the Grammar School. I have always understood that the right was with Reading boys; at all events they, to my knowledge, asserted their right by periodically having a match at cricket there. On these occasions (sometimes not without a fight for it) the Doctor's boys withdrew, having previously driven in stout pegs which stood a little above the surface, but so as not to attract attention; this had the effect of tripping up those who ventured to play there. Mr. Havell, father of the present artist of that name, drew a picture about the year 1816, which gave a faithful representation of the Doctor's play-ground and pupils. From time immemorial this disputed play-ground was at Michaelmas Fair wholly covered with cheese; I have always understood that it was the largest cheese fair in the Kingdom. All the other parts of the Forbury, with the exception of a small meadow then encircled by a semi-circular ditch (supposed to have been formed to aid in the defence of Reading when besieged during the Civil War), but now incorporated with the Public Gardens, was the only Fair Ground we had. Within the Abbey Ruins, and where now stand the houses in the Abbots Walk, was a large garden having blocks of the ruins lying about, and on it a seminary for young ladies conducted by Mrs. Curties. The whole of this property on the Forbury side was enclosed with high gates and wall of flint. On the south side of the Abbey Arch there was a silk manufactory of many years standing, but it became useless in consequence of Legislative enactments in Huskinson's time, and not many years since St. Lawrence's National Schools were erected on its site.

As I have referred to the Abbey I may as well state now what I know about it. Before the present gaol was built there was a good sized meadow between the great hall of the Abbey (where the National Schools of that period were situate), over which were lying large blocks of the ruins, and about the year 1810 or 1811 there were two members of the Society of Friends, living in the upper part of London Street, who used to preach in the Abbey Ruins. One of these was a Mr. Rickman, a relative, I believe, of George Rickman, so well and so recently known to most of us, and also an eccentric Mr. Draper, schoolmaster (into whose care I was at this time committed). One day I was amusing myself amongst the ruins and gathering wallflowers (of which there was a great abundance growing out of the walls), when I saw a lot of the prisoners, dressed in yellow and blue, digging round a tall piece of the ruins with the evident intention of pulling it down, for they very soon brought horses from the timber carriages close by, and with strong chains tried hard to bring it down, but it resisted all their efforts. At this moment other men were forming a road from the main one in the Forbury as an approach to the National Schools, which had then been recently erected within the Abbey walls, and was intended for the children from all three parishes. My attention was suddenly drawn to these men, as those engaged with the horses had left their work, and with Mr. Eastaff, the Governor of the gaol, and Tucker, the turnkey (who had charge of the prisoners, and who kept them in awe with a loaded blunderbuss), were gathered round the men forming the road. I also went to the spot and saw the labourers had found something of interest, which proved to be a stone coffin, supposed to be that of Henry the First. Unfortunately the clumsy fellows broke the stone in two. I have no means of reference, but from my recollection of the event the coffin had ornamental columns all round the outer edge, the latter being about three inches thick, and these were broken to within a few inches of a little moulding at the base. I cannot be mistaken in this, for the coffin was placed in the boys' schoolroom near the master's desk, where I saw it many times afterwards, but by degrees its appearance was altered, as I think, by people, probably Catholics, who were always anxious to take away some fragment from the Abbey. About a year since the Vicar of St. Lawrence requested me to shew him the spot, as near as I could, where this interesting relic was found. I, in consequence, accompanied the rev.

17

gentleman, and placed myself in the same position that I had done nearly 70 years previously, when the coffin was found, and pointed out the spot. Singularly enough the Vicar had a ground plan, which I believe he had himself prepared, and which led him to believe that the said coffin must have been found where I suggested.

About 40 years since I bought a portion of the Abbey Land, and, in digging out the foundation, came upon a block of ruin, probably six feet thick. A hole was cut in it, and with the aid of gunpowder it was blown asunder. It was immediately seen by myself and others that in the centre of the wall there was a yellow deal shaving which had fallen from a plane; it was about three-quarters of an inch in width, curled round, and about three inches in diameter. We attempted to touch it, but in a moment it crumbled into dust. This shaving had probably fallen from the carpenter's bench 700 years ago. On the same spot, and at a depth of about four feet from the present road, the workmen came upon a chapel floor, some of which was covered with tesselated pavement; some of the tiles were broken by the fall of the surrounding flint work, but I thought that the frequenters of St. James' Church would feel interested, and in order that they might view the place more conveniently I had the floor cleaned and a short ladder placed there. In the centre of this floor stood a plain round pedestal of stone, about three feet high and one foot in diameter, with a plinth and a bead at the bottom, and if it were not that the top was perfectly level it would have the appearance of a broken column. No one on seeing it would suppose it to be very ancient. I have this relic at my house now.

On the Sunday when I expected the St. James' people to look at these interesting things, I placed a man of the name of McCarthy, who was well known and himself a Catholic, to take care of the place. After divine service he placed a boy in charge and went home for his dinner; on his return every vestige of the floor had disappeared, to my great grief. The houses No. 7 and 8, Abbot's Walk stand on the exact spot.

Between 50 and 60 years since there were several interesting old buildings in the town, viz., a continuation of similar buildings from the unique old one in the Market Place to the Catherine Wheel Hotel in Friar Street, now Gregory & Co. The corner house opposite St. Lawrence's Church was occupied by a widow of the name of Higgs, who carried on the business of hair dresser, &c., with the assistance of

18

the late Mr. William Golding, who became a valued officer of the Corporation. An assistant of the name of Brown robbed a gentleman of his pocket book whilst attending him, and for his offence he was whipped at the cart's tail. Higgs and Ford, upholsterers, &c., carried on their business at the adjoining house, and when the former retired Ford's people took the house in the Market Place, formerly Marsh's Bank, rendered notorious by its failure and paying nothing. The whole of these houses came to grief about the time I refer to, during a tempest, when the roofs gave way and a pinnacle was blown off St. Lawrence's tower and also a pinnacle off St. John's Church, which church had only then been recently built by the Rev. Francis Trench. This injury to the houses led to their being rebuilt with the corner rounded as you now see it. Opposite the south entrance to St. Lawrence's Church stood a house called the Compter, where lived Davis, the Chief Constable, whose house encroached on the road and nearly reached Knolly's Vault, which lies underneath the carriage way; this building was removed and the corner rounded as it now is. On the opposite side and incorporated with the Church and old Piazza, or 'Church Walk,' there was a cell for the custody of offenders taken during the night.

To revert to the existing old house in the Market Place, this was a pastry cook's shop, the proprietor being a Mr. Millard. Here it was that 'Nice New,' immortalized by 'The Stranger in Reading,' bought his cakes; when this poor fellow died he left all his savings (which I was informed amounted to £300) to Mr. Millard. I remember this man perfectly, and have seen him many a time in the Forbury selling his cakes to the local Militia, who used to drill there before Waterloo; the soldiers amused themselves by pretending to steal his cakes. I have also a vivid recollection of 'Russ,' the milkman, whose portrait is faithfully drawn in the book quoted. About the year 1811 or 1812 I was standing with my father near the *Mercury* office, when a man was placed in the pillory, which stood in a central part of the Market Place, for some offence; and the people threw eggs at him, many missing. I saw Mr. Moody, the coach proprietor, bring two baskets of eggs from Mr. Millard's (before spoken of), and he threw so well that the poor fellow, whose head and arms were fixed, was literally covered with yolks of eggs and other matter, and to complete the affair he was bespattered with refuse from Hiscock's slaughter house. I don't know what his offence was.

19

'Nice New' - the old man who used to sell cakes around the Market Place and Forbury.

Another of these old houses stood opposite the north end of the Upper Ship Inn, and was so close to it that only one vehicle at a time could pass. On Saturdays and fair days it was usual to place a constable there to regulate the traffic. This house corbelled over and was occupied by a hair dresser of the name of Brown. It was a joke with his customers (I was informed) to say that from his upper windows he could shake hands with the girls opposite.

One other of these quaint old houses stood opposite Mr. Hounslow's, and was occupied by Mr. Horniman, umbrella manufacturer. He was a member of the Society of Friends, and during the war in the Peninsula frequently called at our house, and from there adjourned to a large room where the *Times* newspaper was usually read aloud.

Mr. Horniman called frequently upon my father and was very kind to me. He used to admire my canaries, and he said 'I should like to buy one of your young birds to make a present.' I sold him one for 5/-, and as time passed he often said 'Thy bird don't sing, William.' I expressed my regret. At last he said 'I think thee has taken me in.' This was a little too much for my pride, and I saucily said I thought his people were not fond of music. I lost Mr. Horniman's patronage from that moment, and was punished by my Pater by having the rest of my birds taken from me.

— 2 —
St. Giles' Parish 1810-1824

St. Giles' Parish and church - changes in London Street.

As I have been alluding to events which occurred in St. Giles' parish within my memory, I may mention that the first vicar that I knew was the Rev. Mr. Eyre, who succeeded the Hon. and Rev. Mr. Cadogan at the close of the last century. Mr. Cadogan was very popular as an Evangelical and extempore preacher, and drew large congregations. It seems that the new vicar, Mr. Eyre, was a man of a different school from that of his predecessor, and his preaching was not in harmony with the notions of the leading members of the church. This led to a split, and the disaffected bought the old gaol in Castle Street, which they demolished, and built the present church - St. Mary's Episcopal Chapel - on its site. Most of the promoters of this movement I remember, notably Mr. Maberly, who lived in the old house in the London Road, afterwards rebuilt by General Broderick (an old Waterloo officer), and which finally became the residence of our late esteemed townsman, Mr. George May. There were also Mr. French, Dr. Ring, Mr. Lawrence, of Belle Vue, and Mr. Tanner, the brewer, of Castle Street (now Messrs. Blandy and Hawkins); with many others I could mention, as well as Mr. Billing, sen., who erected the new church. This movement induced Dr. Barry, who was at this period chaplain at the gaol, to write a pamphlet, in which he described them as a new sect of Dissenters, and strongly condemned their conduct. I remember that Lady Huntingdon's hymns were sung there. The Rev. Mr. Eyre died about the year 1815. There was a considerable interval before a new vicar was appointed, and it was supposed by many that a son of Dr. Valpy would obtain the living, but in the year 1816 the Rev. Henry Duckenfield (afterwards Sir Henry) obtained the appointment. During the interval after the death of the Rev. Mr. Eyre and the appointment of the new vicar, a gentleman named Dr. Creggon officiated at St. Giles' Church, his residence being in Portland Place, as the deceased vicar's daughters had not left the vicarage. At this time a rather unpleasant incident occurred. A man of

22

the name of Woodeson, who was in the employ of the late Mr. Stephens, at the Mill Lane Brewery, had died; the man was much respected, and his fellow-workmen had arranged to attend the funeral, but by some mismanagement considerable delay occurred. At last the Doctor lost all patience and went home to his dinner; soon afterwards the funeral arrived at the church, and the coffin was placed on the tressells in the middle of the aisle; messengers were sent to the Doctor, but he refused to return, and after long waiting and the expression of much indignation, the mourners and their friends returned to their homes, leaving the coffin in the church the whole night.

Soon after this the Rev. Mr. Duckenfield came into residence. He found that there was a strong feeling against Church rates; and an indisposition to allow him to make some extensive alterations in the church. Numerous meetings and stormy debates occurred in the vestry which induced me to think that this was not quite the place for such animated discussion. Before the decease of the Rev. Mr. Eyre, St. Giles' Churchyard projected over the roadway in Horn Street, and there was a path running from the north-west corner of Church Street to the north-west corner in Horn Street, but by the enlargement of the church this was stopped. The alteration consisted in repewing and the erection of a north gallery. Anterior to this, there was a gallery over the chancel, which was removed and the chancel enlarged. The churchwardens, Messrs. John Yard Willats and Mr. Frankland, of the Crown Hotel, erected new iron railing to the south and west fronts of the churchyard. Up to this period there was an excellent choir led by Mr. Thomas Willats, who formerly had much to do with the musical arangements for Lord Barrymore at Wargrave. All went smoothly for a time, but it eventually became known that the new vicar contemplated the introduction of an organ. From that moment the choir refused their services. The sexton tried to lead the congregational singing; as, however, he had neither voice nor ear for music, he made an awful hash of it. At this time I and another boy, about as old as myself (who is still living), were for our age tolerably good players on the flute, and were studying music under the same master. This became known to the vicar at the time we were both under examination for confirmation, and at his request and with the permission of our parents we selected some of the best voices we could obtain from boys belonging to the Sunday Schools. We were not long before the boys sang well enough to occupy the gallery which the choir had abandoned, my friend and I accompanying

23

them on our instruments. I recollect two tunes which were especial favourites, viz., 'Denmark' and 'Eaton,' the latter having a duet of eight bars for two treble voices, which were really well sung by two of the youngest boys. This state of things lasted until the new organ was erected.

In 1819 and 1820 a new burying ground, situate on the west side of Horn Street and opposite the Church, was consecrated by the Bishop of Oxford, at which ceremony I was present. Burials continued here until some twenty years afterwards, when the cemetery was opened. There are hundreds of our parishioners lying here, amongst them my father, two sons and a daughter. I had not long since visited the place, and was much pained to see the dilapidated state of the tombs of some I knew, and whose descendants, at least many of them, are still living amongst us; how different, I thought, is our cemetery, which although not kept in perfection, forms a perfect contrast, for here loving and sympathising friends are constantly employed in decorating the graves of their departed relations with wreaths and flowers as a tribute of affection. But in the churchyard referred to sheep are pastured. If these remarks should produce any response, it would be easy enough to plant a few shrubs and to have the grass cut and carried away, also to make the place easier of access. I fear that the churchwardens have no funds which they could apply to this purpose.

From the close proximity of my father's residence to the old Blue Coat School, I have a very vivid recollection of it, and of the figures of a couple of scholars perched in two recesses of the front wall, and which have only taken their departure to a more elevated sphere during the last thirty years, viz., to Castle Hill. Brunswick House, now the Blue School, erected by Mr. Reynard, who during my early school days had an excellent establishment in Castle Street, afterwards conducted at the new house.

The first pupil from the old School that I remember was a Sonning lad, whose name was Mulford, son of a widow who kept the Horn Inn there. He was in my father's employ from about the year 1806 until 1817, and became a very skilful mechanic. The Master of the School was a Mr. William May, who died in January, 1812, and was buried in St. Giles' Churchyard with Masonic honours. I followed the procession and heard the funeral service read by the late Dr. Barry. The effect is not likely ever to be forgotten by me.

The head boy at that time was of the same name as the Master; he was son of a confidential servant in the employ of the late Mr. Monck, M.P., of Coley Park. This lad became a clerk in the service of the late Mr. Andrewes, senior, solicitor, living in the Forbury, and I think Town Clerk at that time. This young fellow afterwards became Magistrates' Clerk for several years, and subsequently left Reading to join a firm of solicitors. I have not heard of him since. He need not have left his office had he not made himself disagreeably familiar with the magistrates. It is due, however, to his memory to state that we have not had a more efficient clerk in my time than this Blue Boy.

The late Mr. May was succeeded by Mr. Paget as Master, and he was frequently at our house, which was very near the School. I remember a son of his who was an officer in the King's Service; he was a very gentlemanly fellow, and during a visit to Reading about the year 1816 or 1817, I had the pleasure of accompanying him in a chaise to Streatley, where we dined at the Bull Inn, kept by Mr. Adey, whose good port wine was a great attraction for the undergraduates from Oxford.

At this village we saw Sir Samuel Sheppard, whose residence was at this place. This gentleman was either Attorney-General or Solicitor-General at the time Hardy, Horne Took, Thelwall and others were tried by Lord Ellingborough for high treason. He, it was stated, was very deaf, and always used an ear trumpet in Court, 'but never missed a thing.' Mr. Paget continued Master of the Blue Coat School for several years.

Mr. Rosser succeeded Mr. Paget and retired in 1840. There were some pupils who in after life did honour to this establishment, many of whom sought their fortune in America or our Colonies; others remained, and were either taught trades or became clerks in various offices. Two pupils whom I knew were placed at the *Mercury* office, and because the Amateur Society omitted to send them tickets these young clerks wrote a damaging critique upon the Society's Concert which gave great offence, but the Editor denied all knowledge of it.

25

In after years Mr. Lovejoy said that the offensive paragraph was written and inserted by him and his friend, unknown to the Proprietors. We know of Mr. Lovejoy's honourable career, and as to his friend he informed me that after leaving the *Mercury* office he, by his energy and force of character, became a partner in the firm of one of the most influential journals out of London; and I have recently been informed that he has served the office of Mayor three times in the borough in which he resides.

It will be noticed that there has been a considerable alteration in the level of the streets in this parish, as may be seen at the house at the north-west corner of Bath Court in London Street, the ground floor of which is about three feet lower than the pavement. A few years since two houses near the police station were in a similar position. About the year 1813, London Street was newly paved with York stone, a work at that time much needed and the execution of which was accelerated by the severe criticism of the 'Stranger in Reading.' At this time the upper part of London Street near Church Street was lowered nearly two feet, and the ballast thus removed was used to raise the lower part, the effect of which resulted in the burying of the lower floor of the old houses at the bottom of London Street and rendering it necessary to fix additional steps to the houses higher up, as for instance at Dr. Shettle's, the house in which Lord Sidmouth was born; also at Mr. Moxhay's, which at this time was occupied by Dr. Widows Golding; and at Mr. Oliver Maurice's, where lived Mrs. Mestayre, the friend of Dr. Valpy and Dr. Barry before alluded to. An attempt was made, I believe, to lower the upper part of the street near the Crown Hotel, but this work was stopped in consequence of the workmen coming upon an arch of brickwork, which turned out to be a wine cellar beloning to the hotel, and into which I went; it seemed to run in the direction of the 'Anchor' corner.

In Horn Street a similar raising of the road has buried the lower floor of the corner house in Mill Lane. A much respected old gentleman of the name of Pecover, a confidential clerk to the grandfather of the late Mayor, Mr. Blackall Simonds, and whose portrait used to hang up in the counting house of the Brewery, told me, when I was at the place more than 50 years since, that prior to the erection of the Bear Hotel he had often been obliged in flood time to use a punt in Bridge Street. I have myself seen Mill Lane and Stephens' Brewhouse-yard under water.

To revert again to the Crown Hotel, I may mention that the old house projected and narrowed the carriage way in the time of Mr. or Mrs. Tudor, but this I get by tradition. I, however, remember the front of the hotel being entirely re-built and set back to its present position. Opposite is a spacious yard in which political meetings used to be held. Here I have heard addresses by Sir Francis Burdett, Earl Radnor (then Lord Folkstone), Dr. Lushington, Mr. Monck, Talfourd, Harry Marsh and other celebrities. Here it was that I first heard Fysh Palmer address a meeting; it was during the latter part of the life of George the Third, and when Mr. Palmer first offered himself to the electors. I remember that it was a gloomy day, for Mr. Marsh said that happily there was not a single yard of sky blue to be seen - alluding to the colours of his opponents. Fysh Palmer said: 'Gentlemen, do you think if I were your member that I would vote for six thousand a year to be given to the Duke of Cumberland to visit his Royal Father?' In 1817 I saw Queen Charlotte and Princess Augusta change horses at the Crown Hotel on their way to Bath, and very shortly afterwards the Princess Charlotte, only daughter of the Prince Regent, died, to the great grief of the whole nation. Opposite the Crown, at the time of an election at which Charles Shaw-Lefevre, the father of Lord Eversley, was returned, I was placed at a window where I could with safety see the procession. I think this was in 1812. At length the hon. member arrived with his friends, accompanied by a lot of garland women and a band of music. As was the custom with successful candidates, he threw silver money to the people who followed him, and they scrambled and fought for it. Here Mr. Lefevre delivered his final throw of cash, and a three-shilling piece came through the window of the room in which I was standing, which I pocketed as a souvenir of the occasion.

Opposite St. Giles' Schools in the London Road where the new houses stand, just beyond the old-fashioned overhanging one, was a large coach manufactory commanding the whole of this frontage, including Barnes and Son's premises, and having a frontage in London Street. Here the proprietor (Mr. Cottrell) carried on an extensive business, particularly in post-chaise and stage-coach building, and where now stand the house, stables, &c., of Mrs. Targett, he had a large meadow.

There is a spring of water, called the Conduit, situate near Highgrove which was supposed by the credulous to possess medicinal properties, because from this source the Abbey had been supplied with water; and in confirmation of this a lead pipe in a perfect condition was found in cutting the new straight channel below High Bridge, by which the navigation of the Kennet was greatly improved, and this pipe was supposed to be part of that originally used as stated.

I remember that in the year 1810 the Lancastrian School in Southampton Street was built, and in the following year the children were paraded down London Street with the usual demonstrations of joy. David Fenton, Esq., a gentleman then living in Castle Street, appeared to take great interest in this movement; but since his time the name of the school has been changed to the 'British School.' If I mistake not, the gentleman here referred to was great-grandfather of the Allnatts of the present day.

I have already alluded to the unfortunate dissension in St. Giles' Church which the appointment of Mr. Eyre occasioned, and the secession of most of its principal members, who eventually bought the old gaol in Castle Street and built on its site the present Episcopal Church. One of these was a Mr. P. French, a zealous Christian, whose name has recently been brought to my mind by a reader of the *Observer*, who resides in Oxfordshire, and who writes to me as follows:- 'I have read with much pleasure, in the *Observer*, some interesting particulars given by you on Reading 70 years ago, in which you mention the names of two gentlemen in whom I am interested, viz., the late Mr. P. French and Dr. Ring.' My correspondent was good enough to send me a printed circular, from which I make the following interesting extract; it is dated 10th April, 1856: 'Peppard, Oxon. About 65 years ago the Honourable and Rev. Mr. Cadogan was preaching the Gospel of Christ at St. Giles' Church, Reading, with great power and the most delightful success. ... Among the numerous converts given to that eminent man were some who felt most deeply for the spiritual darkness and destitution of the surrounding villages. The secluded village of Peppard, remarkable for its lovely scenery, was, with its neighbouring hamlets, in a fearful state of heathenism and immorality. This state of things aroused the zealous efforts of a band of Christian men. One of them, a Mr. Peter French, of Reading . . . . . . although a churchman, with admirable largeness of

28

heart, built at Peppard a chapel at his own expense, and for thirty years contributed fifty pounds per annum towards the support of a minister.'

The Mr. French here spoken of was universally beloved; his son, who was educated by Dr. Valpy, became a popular clergyman in the Church of England, and I believe he has left a son who is also a church minister. Mr. P. French's son married a daughter of Dr. Valpy.

Another Oxfordshire reader of the *Observer* writes: 'I have read with much interest the valuable information given by you on Reading 70 years ago. There are two gentlemen named whose sterling qualities and true Christian character should not be overlooked, and of whom I should like to hear much more, Dr. Ring and Mr. P. French; the latter exactly 90 years ago built, at his own expense, a chapel at Peppard, and for 30 years paid an annual endowment of fifty pounds. Dr. Ring was an intimate friend of Mr. French, and they frequently drove over together to attend the service at Peppard Chapel. The first appointed minister was the Rev. Joseph Walker, which appointment occurred in the year 1798.'

I have heard that the Rev. F. Trench, who, I believe, was brother to the late Archbishop of Dublin, has recently died, and I am, therefore, inclined to trespass a few remarks which occur to me at this moment, in reference to this excellent but in one sense singular gentleman. I was present at St. Giles' Church when first Mr. Trench took part in the service, the Rev. Henry Duckenfield, the vicar, preaching the sermon. The effect on my mind in hearing the curate read was: I wonder if this clergyman, who has the repute of being an excellent scholar, was ever taught to read. Positively he seemed to have no control of his voice, and this peculiarity for a time and until we became used to it was not only painful, but counteracted all sense of devotional feeling; and this peculiarity increased with advancing years. Nevertheless, he was an excellent Christian gentleman and deservedly beloved in Reading. Mr. F. Trench lived at the next house to my own residence, then 26, London Street, but now, I think, 54 (during the whole time of his curacy), with the late Mr. and Mrs. Clacy, parents of the late Reading Postmaster. Upon one occasion I offended the rev. gentleman in this way. He had taken the house, No. 1, Southern Hill, and at that time I had occasion to call on him. The house had previously been occupied by Mr. Willimott, a gentleman of great taste, who not only substituted plate glass to the windows, but made a nice lawn at the back, with flower beds, &c. Mr. Trench asked me into his study, which commanded a view of the said garden. He remarked 'I thought to have found the garden in much better order, &c.' This was too much for me, for I had paid for the work done to it; so I remarked that he had employed some indifferent gardeners since I last saw the place. 'In what way, pray?' 'Why, you have Cochin cocks and hens running all over the garden scratching holes, and on the centre of the lawn a hen coop and a lot of chickens.' To these inconsiderate remarks of mine he angrily replied that he was not to be dictated to as to how he should manage his poultry. To revert again to Mr. Willimott, he formed a small lake in front and cut vistas through the plantation; he also, by permission of the late Mr. Wm. Watlington, of our town, cut similar openings through the plantation of Redlands, now the property of our popular townsman, Mr. William Palmer. The effect of these openings was unique, for from the drawing room window he commanded a view of the valley of the Thames, both east and west, the Oxfordshire hills, Sonning, and the hills at Wargrave and Henley.

As the property at Southern Hill is now in the possession of Mr. George Palmer, it may interest his family to have a sort of reflex of what it was 45 years ago. At the time of the erection of our hospital, Mr. Henry Briant, the architect of it, was about to build for me the house (lately the residence of Mr. Roslin, and now the property of Mr. George Palmer), in the King's Road, called Swiss Villa. Mr. Willimott said 'I once built a house at Clapham Rise which was to cost £4,500, but in the end I paid £10,000 for it'; adding 'most gentlemen build a house once in their lives, but seldom venture on a second.' He gave me a rough plan of his house, from which I built, in miniature, Swiss Villa.

I did not very often see Mr. Trench after the time to which I have above referred until he one day came from the Hospital towards Eldon Square, and seeing me he waved his hand in a friendly manner, and I responded by raising my hat. In doing so I let fall some cigars which Capt. Montagu gave me just before, and Mr. Trench, seeing that I was disconcerted, picked up some of them for me, and remarked 'Never mind Mr ____, I am as fond (or used to be) of smoking as you are.'

In a former paper I alluded to the erection of a new Chapel at the upper part of London-street, which is now known as St. Giles' Hall. Prior to its erection there was a small place of worship near the present structure, which was frequented by a very unobtrusive sect, who, I suppose, were not fond of music, for I never heard a note from that quarter, although I lived within fifty yards of them. I am alluding to about the year 1810. I, as a child, had the impression that it was a branch of the Society of Friends, and I still retain that opinion.

About this period there lived a very eccentric old gentleman near the Meeting House above referred to, who had property adjoining, which included the two houses now known as 122 and 124, London Street, as also a house and garden in the rear. I am referring to a Mr. Brookman, who, with his wife, I believe, frequented this place of worship. Mrs. Brookman dressed in similar costume to that of the Society of Friends. For some years prior to his decease Mr. Brookman had his coffin made, which he kept in a room, and when the state of the weather would not permit his amusing himself in the garden he sought exercise indoors by polishing it. At his death he bequeathed a sum of money to the Green Girls' School. This singular old gentleman is buried in St. Giles' Churchyard, a few feet from the gate as you enter from Church Street, on the right-hand side, and close to the old path which ran diagonally into Horn Street. There is a large flat stone over the vault which I last saw in the year 1822, and I think if the grass which has grown over it were removed the following inscription would be found on it:- 'T.B., well-wisher to the Green Girls' Charity.'

At the lower end of London Street, before the opening was made for the formation of the Queen's Road, there were three old houses, which were taken down to enable the approach to be formed. These were severally occupied by Mr. Hallows, silk manufacturer, Mr. Greenwood, butcher (afterwards Johnson), and Mr. Holloway, blacksmith. On the south side of the Black Horse Inn, where now are gates, was a right of way to what is now known as Vine Court but in 1814 as Elkins' Buildings, and which at that period presented a totally different aspect to what it does now, and was of greater extent, particularly on the north side of this block of buildings. Here was also a substantial house occupied by Humphreys, barge master; also one on the south side by Mr. Brooker, plasterer, who retired from business at

31

the completion of the Bear Hotel, about the year 1811, and eventually ended his days in a detached residence in Clackman's Fields, Whitley. At the south end of Elkins' Buildings, there was a large schoolroom occupied by that gentleman for the education of boys. Mr. Elkins and his family resided in the house now in the possession of Mr. Stevens, upholsterer, Nos. 17 and 19, London Street. After the death of Mr. Elkins, which occurred in 1814, the schoolroom was taken for a time by the Wesleyans; this I remember from the fact of my sister, who was my senior by nine years, having taken me there to hear a popular preacher, of the name of Waterhouse.

At the decease of Mr. Elkins, his son converted the dwelling house in London Street, which was a private residence, into a stationer's shop, and carried on this business for some years. The Rev. Mr. Duckenfield (afterwards Sir Henry), Vicar of St. Giles', lodged in this house during the repairs at the Vicarage and his recovery from a serious attack of fever. Mr. Elkins, for a short period, became a Parish and Vestry Clerk, and probably would have continued to hold that office, but for the following untoward circumstance. One of his servants in the night suddenly aroused him; and he died immediately of apoplexy. He left a widow, and a son who was a lieutenant in the Navy, of whom I know not the end, but Mrs. Elkins finished her days in one of the Southampton Street Almshouses.

The Queen's Road was formed under the superintendence of the late Mr. J.J. Cooper, Architect and Surveyor (father of Mr. J.O. Cooper), and until this work was executed Gunter's Brook ran, as an open stream, through Mr. Elkins' premises and Mr. Brooker's garden to the Kennet. East Street did not extend beyond South Street, but simply a narrow path gave access to the back of the London Street houses. All the surrounding land consisted mainly of two deep pits, with a house in the west one, occupied by the noted Jerry Tibble. The two pits were used by boys for cricket; and a road ran between them to Blandy Wharf, Star Lane. The lower part of South Street has been lowered some ten feet. Near the 'Six Bells,' a Mr. Hill had a boat-house, where he constructed barges of 120 tons burden, and launched them into the Kennet by means of a dock. Mr. Hill had an extensive business in the timber trade, and was brother-in-law to Mr. Boult, who for years held these pits until the gravel was exhausted. Before railways were introduced there was a very prosperous coach-building manufactory, particularly for post-chaises,

St^t. GILES'S CHURCH *in* READING.

St. Giles' church, where Darter was christened on 22 January 1804.

carried on close to High Bridge, west side, where now there is a public-house, and opposite the magistrates' office, the proprietor being Mr. Phelps, who built it as his private residence. It is now converted into a chemist's shop.

To continue my remarks on this part of Reading (near the Crown Inn) where I first saw the light, many important improvements have occurred, particularly on the west side, but very few opposite. Up to about the year 1814 there were at the London Street entrance to the Unitarian Chapel two very old houses with small shop windows, which were probably built in the reign of Elizabeth. These, as also the small Chapel I have referred to, were the property of Mr. Sims, at that time a builder of repute, whose business premises were in Mill lane. He removed the two old buildings and erected the two modern-style houses and shops with balconies, from one of which Fyshe Palmer made his maiden speech to the Liberals of our Borough in the reign of George the Third.

It is a singular fact that no attempt has been made to widen and otherwise improve the approach to the town from the London Road. Until the year 1833 this was the only entrance to Reading from the east, and from the south also, excepting Southampton Street. At the upper end of London Street four roads meet, and it is unquestionably the most dangerous spot in the town. At this point a few years since a commercial traveller, in driving past it, had his horse so frightened that it ran against the Crown Hotel, dashing the chaise to pieces and killing the unfortunate gentleman.

A large sum of money has been expended in widening streets and rounding corners of the approaches to them, either at the expense of owners, or by the Sanitary Authority; if this policy were judiciously continued, no one, I think, would complain, but to leave any longer untouched this important entrance to its principal street, especially if any further accidents occur, will be considered by all men of thought a serious matter. I invite my fellow-townsmen to inspect the south-west corner, on which stands the Anchor Inn. The London Road at this point is only about twenty feet wide, from kerb to kerb. It will be noticed that opposite the Inn in question stand the newly-arranged schools for both sexes in connection with St. Giles' parish (formerly the Blue Coat

School). Here are being educated about 300 pupils. When these children are dismissed to their homes, they rush out in a playful mood in the road, to the imminent danger of their lives. If it were not for the almost constant attendance of a policeman in this locality, some fearful accidents might have occurred ere this through reckless driving. The improvement I venture to suggest is the removal of the old Coaching Night House, and also the Anchor public-house adjoining. The corner of this Inn has an acute angle, and about six feet from it, across the pavement, is another angle with a lamp-post, which serves the double purpose of a guard to pedestrians and a rubbing post for the unwashed loungers, of whom there are usually too many at this point. It is a question of compensation, I apprehend, and the best way of making the suggested improvement would be by removing the Anchor Inn altogether, for there are at least eight other inns, or beer-houses, within a radius of about 150 yards; or the thing might be done by paying a certain amount to the present proprietors and let them set back any new structure, so as to meet the requirements of the public. A short time since one of our spirited townsmen, at his own cost, removed one of the oldest but notoriously bad houses from the west side of London Street, as also a cottage in its rear of a similar character. In its place, shops of a superior kind have been erected, which greatly improve this part of the street.

I cannot dismiss my remembrance of this old inn, now destroyed, without stating that I remember it as the *Goat,* afterwards as the *Lamb,* and during the Peninsula War it was the headquarters of the 'Buffs' recruiting party. In the autumn of 1814, when the allied Sovereigns supposed that they had finally disposed of Napoleon, and our Government was so imprudent as to reduce the Army, Sergt. Philips, of the Blues, having obtained his discharge, took this house and gave it the name of the 'Duke of Wellington.' Waterloo followed, and its anniversary in 1816 was celebrated by the Foot Guards on these premises.

Since I described the existence of one or two dissenting congregations in the neighbourhood of the old Crown Hotel, it has occurred to me that I have forgotten to mention one of small proportions, who had a meeting house up a court in Silver Street. I think they were Primitive Methodists, or a humble portion of St. Giles' congregation, who left the Church after the death of the Hon. and Rev.

Mr. Cadogan. I knew two of those who attended this chapel at a very early period, one a person named Weller, and another of the name of Salt, a sawyer at one time in our employ. He was a very religious man, and did much good amongst the poor at a time when the drum and fife and much drink were the order of the day, particularly in Silver Street, from which locality many recruits were procured. Probably the man Salt is remembered by some of the older inhabitants.

To revert once more to the Unitarians and their new place of worship, I may mention that when very few in number they assembled in part of Mr. Sims' premises in Mill Lane. Afterwards, by the clever preaching of their Ministers, the congregation increased considerably, and consisted of some of the upper stratum of the middle class.

I have no idea how it was that the Unitarians gave up their place of worship. It probably occurred at the death of Mr. Sims, the proprietor. They now have a much more commodious chapel on the Redlands Estate, the Rev. R. Rodolph Suffield being their pastor.

It is amusing to reflect on the changes which have occurred at this place since the demolition of the old chapel, as also in its immediate neighbourhood, such as the closing of the old Crown Posting Inn, and its conversion into shops. The new chapel of the Unitarians became a place for meetings of a miscellaneous character. The excellent bowling green which was for a long period connected with the Hotel, and supported by the leading men of the town, in close proximity to the building used as the said chapel. In the summer there was usually a large attendance, and in the event of a storm the members had a sort of Swiss cottage to shelter them, or, as often happened, to play a rubber at whist. About the year 1824, the members of the club met for the first time that season to play a match. Suddenly a great noise sprang up, which we could not account for, and it was of such a character that our game was suspended, until Charles, the waiter from the Crown, explained that a new set of worshippers had taken the chapel, but their name had not transpired. The noise consisted of shouting by the men, screaming by the women, as also jumping by them all; this noise on the floor had the effect produced by a lot of soldiers marching on the boards. The whole thing could only be compared to the feeding time at Wombwell's Menagerie. We were glad when they disappeared. It was suggested that probably these people were the same as those elsewhere described as having closed their places of business and retired to Tilehurst Common to witness the end of the world, the dissolution of which one of their leaders predicted would occur that day.

— 3 —
St. Mary's Parish 1810 - 1826

St. Mary's Parish and church - the Oracle - murder of Father Longuet.

In the year 1811 there was a 'Commercial and Classical School' in Chain Street, where, at this time (1885), the Reading Dispensary stands, and it was conducted by two brothers (Messrs. W. and Thos. Church). These gentlemen died many years since, and were interred in a vault near the entrance to St. Mary's Vicarage.

In the autumn of the above year I was placed at this school, and remained there until the end of 1818. Talfourd, afterwards one of our judges, was a pupil, but he left the following year for the much more popular school of Dr. Valpy. At this period Archdeacon Nares was Vicar of St. Mary's, but I knew little of him excepting that he took a great interest in promoting the education of the humbler classes, and providing national schools for both sexes, such schools being built in the Abbey Ruins, and being then the only National Schools for the whole town; I also remember that he was supposed to be the author of an inscription for the tombstone of the deceased sexton, A. Deane, who was much respected, and although this memorial has for a long period disappeared, I retain the following in my memory:
> 'Here once I stood where thou dost now,
> And viewed the dead as thou dost me,
> E're long shalt thou lay full as low,
> And others stand and look on thee.'

A. Deane was buried about the year 1811 on the south side of the churchyard.

At this time there were only two paths through the churchyard and a carriage drive to the vicarage; the paths formed a cross and ran from Chain Street to the south-west corner and from Minster Street to the

'Butts'; this left the south quarter towards Gun Street as an open space for the recreation of children. My belief is that A. Deane was almost the first person buried in that quarter. A Mr. James had a house and shop in the churchyard, and when it became necessary to enlarge the burying ground this was demolished, and it was stated that Mr. James was buried in his own cellar. There was also a house on the south side with the back of it opposite Messrs. Hart and Sons, and there were trees in front of this residence corresponding with those opposite the Dispensary; all these trees 72 years since were quite hollow and seemed to entirely exist by the bark through which the sap ascended. I threw a boy's cap in the one opposite the Dispensary in 1812, and had to obtain the assistance of a man with a ladder to recover it. Last spring I saw that this tree bore leaves as fresh and green as it did nearly three quarters of a century since.

In the year 1816, the two houses referred to, viz., the one occupied by Mr. James and the other in which a Mr. Martin lived, were pulled down and all trees and other obstructions removed. A ditch which ran parallel with Gun Street by its whole length, was cleaned out, and Messrs. Wilder and Son fixed the iron railing in 1816. This portion of the churchyard was thus properly fenced in, but in effecting this great improvement it became necessary to raise the road considerably, the effect of which may be seen by looking at the Shades Inn, and until recently the Cross Keys Inn was at a similar depth below the carriage road. At that time there were attached to the Shades Inn a lock-up for the detention of prisoners during the night, but this I believe was removed at the time of the sale of the Oracle. The latter was evidently built at a time when this road was several feet lower down than now, and I perfectly recollect that the centre yard was easy of access for heavy carriages, and there was a pair of massive oak gates which could easily be shut; the date on these was 1628; they are now the property of Mr. Alderman Hewett, and may be seen at his private residence, Downshire Road.

It is not without pain that I have introduced the subject of the Oracle, for it revives in my memory early associations, and brings to the front the fact that Reading has lost a most valuable and princely gift, for not only did it include the Oracle but also other estates. It seems that Mr. Kendrick, the donor, was a successful manufacturer of sail cloth, &c., and having made his fortune in Reading felt anxious that this business should continue after his decease; therefore he either built, or caused to be built, the said Oracle, which was an extensive range of shops and warehouses forming a square with a large court-yard in the centre. It seems to have occurred to him, or to the person who drew his will, that this manufacture might die out, for he introduced a condition that if from any cause this manufacture should cease to exist, the whole of this property should go to Christ's Hospital, London,

In the year 1849, the Lord Chancellor, in severe terms, censured the Reading Corporation, who, he stated, 'had for a long series of years misapplied the funds of John Kendrick's bequest to the town.' He, therefore, affirmed the decree of the Vice-Chancellor, which ordered the transfer of this charity to Christ's Hospital. The abuse of this Kendrick gift must have been palpable to most people, for as far back as 1812 I often, between school hours, wandered about the Oracle with others, and, at that time, the whole mass of building was going to ruin. The centre was a large open space of greensward, with shops all round, but the original manufacture for which the place was intended had gradually died out, and from the period mentioned up to 1818 the only persons who were engaged in business were Messrs. Bartlett, Wolfe, Wainwright, Miles and Jones. A few of the rooms were used by silk weavers and pin makers, also for workshops, and the Minster Street tradesmen used others for stores, lumber, &c. The parish school was here, and was managed by a Mrs. Stokes, whose descendants of the fourth generation still exist in the town. There was also a long rope-walk, which continued to be used until the original buildings were removed.

To return to St. Mary's parish, A. Deane, the respected but now deceased Sexton, was succeeded by Jonathan Prater, who, during the time of the open ground in the south referred to, was a dreadful nuisance to us boys; but a few years later, and soon after the arrival of Dr. Millman, while I was engaged in the Church, he came and asked me to look at a skeleton he had discovered in sinking a grave at the north-west corner of the church-yard (as you enter to the Butts); it seemed perfect, but it had on its legs and wrists, rings with a chain which were attached to a ring in the centre; on inquiry I was informed that this man must have been hung in chains, as the ground where the body lay was for many years appropriated to the burial of those who were executed at Gallows Tree Common. About sixty years since Mr. Goddard, a farmer, living a Lower Earley, pointed out to me the spot where the executions took place, and stated that the culprits were dragged up out of a cart. The gaol at the close of the last century stood where is now the Rev. G.I. Tubbs's Church, and, during its existence as a gaol, all the funerals from it took place at the spot I have indicated; those from the new gaol were interred in the east corner of St. Lawrence's Churchyard. My Pater told me that it was no uncommon thing for the culprit and his attendant to stop at the Oxford Arms, Silver Street, then kept by a man of the name of Fletcher, on their way from the gaol to Gallows Tree Common, and there partake of liquor of some kind.

In the year 1812, as I was passing through Minster Street, I saw a group of persons standing and listening to an account of the assassination of Mr. Percival, the Prime Minister, as he was passing through the lobby of the House of Commons. He who was reading the *Gazette,* in which this murder was narrated, was Mr. Warry, an active Liberal of that day, and he it was who was selected to go to France and endeavour to induce Mr. Monck (who was at the time residing in that country) to return and contest the approaching election against the sitting member, Mr. Simeon. Mr. Warry read aloud the particulars of the assassination, which was committed by a man named Bellingham, because it was supposed he had been disappointed in connection with some government appointment, and who justly paid the extreme penalty of the law for his crime.

While I am describing the parish of St. Mary, I may mention that at this time there was only one house on the south side of the Oxford Road (from about 200 yards from the White Hart corner), and this was occupied by Colonel Balkam, an old Walcherin officer; this house stood in a meadow, now Zinzan Street. From the Oxford Street entrance to Howard Street, to Sydney Terrace, the path was much higher than the road, and there was a row of trees standing there. The south part of the Oxford Road, known as Russell Street, Sydney Terrace (up to Prospect Street), and including Baker Street, was all cultivated by Mr. Swallow as nursery gardens, and there was a large pond at the bottom of Propect Street.

On the north side of Oxford Street, from the Fox Inn stables thence westward, I remember only the New Inn and the turnpike house; all the

41

King Street and Minster Street corner. An umbrella hangs outside the shop of Mr. Horniman, umbrella maker.

land, with slight exceptions, being attached to Battle Farm. About 63 years since, this farm, then in the occupation of Mr. Vines, was wholly destroyed by fire, at which I was present, and which was supposed to have been caused by lightning.

About the year 1812, some houses were erected on the north side of the Oxford Road, a few yards from Broad Street, in one of which a Mrs. Bayley lived; this house caught fire, and the only water that could be obtained was from a pump in West Street. At this time there was a regiment of soldiers in the town, which, I think, was the Buffs, and as soon as the alarm was given the soldiers turned out, and by their officers formed into two lines, the one passing leathern buckets of water, by which the engine was kept at work, and the empty ones passed back by the other line; there was no confusion, and the fire was subdued.

The alarm of fire was usually given by crossing the bells, as it was called, and, where soldiers were, by beating of drums. So it was in this case. In 1818, whilst the Rev. H.H. Millman was preaching, some one pulled off the heavy tenor bell of St. Mary's, which had the effect of stopping the discourse and of emptying the church, every one thinking that a fire had occurred. They said bell had been pulled up and was resting on the stay so that the clock would strike on it; therefore, it did not require much exertion to set it in motion.

Now that I have referred so much to the Oxford Road, I am reminded of a sad event which became known to us at school at an early hour in the morning on February 13th, 1817. Our head boy, James Draper, of Theale, was reading morning prayers, when an old pupil of the Messrs. Church came into the schoolroom very much excited, and stated that he had just heard of the cruel murder of the Roman Catholic Priest (the Rev. Mr. Longuet), whose body had been found with several mortal wounds in it, and was lying on the south side of the road (just beyond where now is the Barracks), and a short distance from the old turnpike, his horse being found in a narrow lane leading to the Thames. From what I remember of the event the rev. gentleman had been to Wallingford on horseback to give lessons, and had received payment for his services up to Christmas of the preceeding year, and it is supposed that the assassin knew something of this, for he was robbed of what money he had. On the day this crime was committed, there had been a pigeon match at Pangbourne, and the supposed murderer had

43

left the shooting party earlier than the others; but owing to his family being of such respectability and long standing in Reading, it was not until about the time of the trial of Queen Caroline that any suspicion attached to him, excepting by one or two of those in the employ of his father. No immediate attention was paid to this rumour. I, however, heard from a man of the name of Rider that he had rescued the supposed murderer from committing suicide by drowning near Blake's Bridge. He soon after died, to the great relief of those who knew his secret. As may be supposed, he was always in trouble and a disgrace to his family. After he had passed away the matter was much spoken of, and eventually an article appeared in a local paper, in which the editor severely censured those who knew who the guilty person was for not making it known, when by doing so they would have relieved many innocent persons from suspicion. For many years after this event there was a short inscription fixed on an elm tree opposite where the crime was committed. I remember that hand-bills were issued, in which a reward of £250 was offered to any one giving information that would lead to the conviction of the offender. At the time of this murder there were two boys at our school who were Roman Catholics, and they seemed dreadfully distressed; their name was Hall. There were but few persons of this religion in Reading at this period; indeed so limited in number were they that a room in Vastern Street was large enough for them to hold their services in. Eventually we had a clergyman who, to my mind, had more eloquence than wisdom, and he was for ever assailing them from the pulpit, and sometimes from the platform. From the time of this crusade the Catholics increased in number, and the outcome is that we have St. James' Church.

To revert again to St. Mary's parish. In the year 1818, Archdeacon Nares was succeeded by the Rev. H.H. Millman, who had the north and west galleries of the church erected. In 1835, the Rev. W. Yates became vicar, and he very greatly improved the church. In 1840 the churchyard was so full of graves that it was with difficulty any spot could be found for more interments; this I should not have known but for the fact that in riding through Gun Street about half-past four in the morning, I saw the grave-digger (whom Mr. Butler, the artist, has immortalised) very busy, spade in hand, chopping up a half decomposed corpse, in order to make room for another grave. I called out to him to desist, which he did, and covered up with earth the remains. This induced me to insert a letter in a local paper, in which I drew public attention to the horrible state of this burying ground; to this the Vicar replied, and the outcome of it all was the present cemetery.

In the year 1862, the Rev. A.P. Purey-Cust became vicar, and great alterations were again made, and the appearance of the church much improved by the removal of the galleries and the enlargement of the chancel. The rev. gentleman was greatly beloved, and it was with deep regret we parted with him from Reading.

It may be of interest to our successors to know that a branch of the Kennet, which at one time I believe was navigable for small boats, passed by the back of the late Mr. Jonathan Tanner's Brewery, under Bridge Street, and discharged itself at High Bridge. I think it was the year 1811 that I saw this brewery on fire, and some of the burning rafters fell into this stream and were taken out of the water by the three brothers, Messrs. Jackson, who were stone masons and whose yard and workshops adjoined the first-named bridge. I always understood that this brook was of great advantage in the time of floods; and I have no knowledge why it was abandoned, or who had the right to fill it in.

In July of the year 1826 the Lord Mayor of London (Venables I believe) with some Aldermen and others paid a visit to Oxford in the State Barge. On their return they visited Reading and made the Bear Hotel their head-quarters. But their barge was moored with its head partly up the said brook near the Lower Ship yard, where there were landing steps, now considerably encroached upon. There is at this time an accumulation of silt where the Lord Mayor's barge was moored, so that no boat could now approach the same spot. On the Lord Mayor's return next day he and his party walked down the path intending to embark near the bridge. The boat had arrived, but for want of ballast could not get under the said bridge. A gentleman on board called out, 'we want the weight of the Corporation to enable us to move.' This caused some merriment and also provoked some severe remarks, not only upon the bridge, but also upon the wretched state of the towing path. The Lord Mayor remarked that 'the name *Silly Bridge* was well chosen.' It is to be regretted that this state of things still remains a blot upon our escutcheon. As the vessel slowly moved under Silly Bridge an accident occurred of a serious character to one of those on board. On the east side of the bridge there were horses waiting to tow the boat, and on the tow line being fastened to the post one of the horses, I think, slipped and so strained it that it broke the post suddenly in two and knocked down one of the gentlemen so violently that he remained unconcious for some time. I never knew the result, but the accident interfered a good deal with the pleasures of the day, which was spent at Cleveden, near Maidenhead. I had the pleasure of being one of the party, and of taking luncheon on the lawn; the refreshments being supplied by Mr. James Tagg, of the Bear Inn, Reading

— 4 —

The War against Napoleon

Reading during the war against Napoleon - recruiting in London Street - prisoners of war brought to Reading - a walk to Ascot to see Marshal Blucher.

No one of my age can forget the year 1811. The comet which appeared at that time was a magnificent spectacle, and continued with us for eight to ten months. If any of my young friends would like to know its form, I may mention that it was very much like an instrument of torture too frequently used in public schools of that day, but to my mind its application never did any good.

This year brought us intelligence of a victory, gained by Wellington over Soult in the Peninsula, and in consequence another illumination occurred of greater splendour than the last, as the inhabitants had by this time become accustomed to these demonstrations, and had provided themselves with appliances for lighting up, which they had not before. I may also mention that many of them had their sense of loyalty somewhat quickened by having their windows broken when they were not illuminated. At this period of the war, and indeed to the end of it, the drum and fife, as also the trumpet-call of the Blues, were constantly heard in London Street, and this was not surprising, for five of the public-houses were taken as head quarters for the recruiting parties, viz., two for the Cavalry and three for the Line. The Black Horse and Barley Mow were for the Blues, into which a man of the name of Birch enlisted; he was killed at Waterloo, his horse having bolted with him into the enemy's lines, where he was cut down. This man's brother kept the Star Inn, near the Police Station, for some years. The 7th Hussars was a very favourite regiment; the Fountain was their rendezvous, and Berris, the son of the landlord enlisted in this Regiment; so also did a son of Mr. Harbour, of the Anchor public-house, opposite the Crown Hotel.

Many distressing events have I witnessed, living as I did so near the scenes I have described. Sometimes it happened that young fellows who came with teams of horses to our market on Saturday would be induced by the recruiting parties to take beer with them, and thereby get enlisted. As soon as the mother or other relatives heard of it, every endeavour was made to get them off by paying 'smart' money; and if not promptly done the recruits were sent off without loss of time to the Depots. One Saturday I saw Mr. Tubb, of Tubb's Farm, London Road, driving his own team home, his carter and a boy of 16 having enlisted.

So great was the pressure for recruits at this period that very unfair means were frequently adopted to get men for the Army. At this time a rather amusing circumstance occurred at the upper part of London Street. A young man in want of work asked some one to assist him on the road. Sergt. Bond, of the Buffs, who was standing near, said 'Here, I will help you,' and very dexterously slipped a shilling into his hand; 'that is,' he added, 'to serve your King and Country, my lad.' The poor fellow immediately dropped the money and made an effort to escape; but the recruiting party surrounded him, and very soon some men and boys joined in the affray. Mr. Restall, a hair-dresser, who had just been engaged in his business at the Crown Hotel, came across the street, and seeing a great disturbance opposite his house, enquired the cause, and as soon as he knew he became interested on behalf of the young man in question. At this moment one of the Bath coaches drove up and stopped at the Anchor corner. Restall being well-known to the coachman, said something to him, and, on returning to the scene, told the poor fellow to break away for the coach; this he, with the assistance of the mob, accomplished, and having jumped up, he was quickly driven away amid cheers from the people, but with loss of temper and a shilling to the soldiers. This is only an example of what was frequently occurring. In addition to the constant excitement to which I have alluded, the Regiment of Blues, which was stationed here, paraded London Street in undress, riding one horse and leading another; but now and then a horse would get away, making it very dangerous. Col. Sir John Elley, who was in command, allowed his band to play in the Forbury sometimes. Two of his men met with an alarming accident, which occurred in this way. They were quartered at the Black Horse, and those who know this part of Reading are aware that the entrance to the side of the said Inn is somewhat similar to that by the side of the ironmonger's shop opposite the Lower Ship. These men on returning home turned down this road towards Crane Wharf and walked into the Kennet at High Bridge. An alarm was at once raised, and Mr. William Blandy's housekeeper, who afterwards became the wife of Mr. Eyre, the mace-bearer, with great presence of mind placed lighted candles in the windows, and the men were happily rescued, although neither could swim. Those were the days of oil lamps, and as those on the bridge were of this kind, they afforded but little assistance. These men I was informed had merely gone to the Post Office, which at the time referred to was kept by Mr. White, opposite Messrs. Cocks and Co.'s Sauce Warehouse in Duke Street. I am sorry to state that one of these fine fellows was taken ill with small-pox and died at the Black Horse Inn. I saw him buried with military honours in St. Giles' Church-yard.

At this period there were many Danish prisoners of war here, some of whom I fear suffered much, for I remember that two of them committed suicide, one at the 'Vasterns,' and another at the Long Barn Inn. A Danish officer, while a prisoner of war here, married a Miss Cooper, of St. Giles' parish (daughter of a retired professional man of that name), and when it was supposed that Napoleon's career was finally closed, these Danish prisoners, before returning to their homes, drew up a memorial and presented it to Mr. Sherwood, of the firm of Hooper and Sherwood, then an eminent surgeon, thanking him for his great kindness and gratuitous professional services during their long captivity.

One day, about the year 1813, I saw a long line of French prisoners escorted down London Street to the Saracen's Head stables where they were put with clean straw to lie down upon; they were formed three or four deep, and presented a very miserable appearance, their clothes being in rags, and shoes nearly worn out; some had knapsacks with small round tins affixed to them; others had scran bags. My impression is that they came from Southampton. I often saw the late Mr. Alderman Herbert Lewis interesting himself on their behalf; and an old gentleman of the name of Terrier, a member of the Society of Friends, who could converse with them in their own language, was often engaged in performing acts of kindness to them. I noticed that the officers (or perhaps they were non-commissioned) often changed five-franc pieces. My interest was concentrated on those prisoners who had procured leg of mutton bones and were busily engaged in carving them into all sorts of little curiosities, such as domino boxes, tobacco stoppers, and many little useful things, which they sold to those who visited them.

During the protracted war in the Peninsula, both by sea and land, no young man could safely go to London. I remember a young fellow of the name of Chandler living in Mount Pleasant, who with another, whose name I have forgotten, went to town for the purpose of working at their business as carpenters and joiners. They had not been there more than a few weeks, when on their way back to their work after dinner they stopped to look into a shop window. A press gang came up and forcibly took them down to the water where they were put into an armed boat and taken down to the Nore. These men fought in several battles on board His Majesty's ships, and after many years Chandler returned home, but his comrade was killed in action. Chandler lived for some years after these events somewhere near his former home; he was well known, and probably some are living who may remember him. My father when a young man was twice 'pressed' and taken to Nore, but being in a Government office was liberated. He told me that when the Press Gang boat shot under London Bridge the people threw brick-bats and stones at them.

I have related these events, of which I have perfect recollection, to shew the straits to which the country was driven at this time. Everything almost was taxed, even light and air. Besides the Press Gang, we had our local Militia, commanded by Lord Blandford, and which consisted principally of trades-people; also the Berkshire Militia, which was nearly as oppressive as conscription. My own father paid eighty pounds for a substitute, and it became necessary to form clubs for mutual protection. To add to our trials there were thrown upon our sympathy many refugees, especially Germans, for whom public subscriptions were raised, and also the proceeds from amateur concerts given on their behalf.

The greatest strain I believe occurred in the year 1814, when there was a severe frost, which lasted for many weeks, and there was positively no coal in the town for some time. Bosier's and Mill's barges were frozen on the Thames, and Whitworth's and Atherton's boats (I think these were the proprietors) were similarly placed on the Kennet; indeed, I think that the navigation of our rivers ceased for about three months. Mr. George's broad-wheeled waggons were in great request, and were the only means by which we obtained goods from London.

The buildings of the *Reading Observer* stand on the site of the offices from which the waggons started. Bricklayers, plasterers, and labourers were in great distress for want of work, and all the necessities of life were at fabulous prices. Yet we were all loyal, with the exception of about a dozen of the inhabitants of insignificant importance, and these we designated Jacobins and avoided them, but I really think that they had not much feeling in the matter, further than that John Bull should not have it all his own way.

As a matter of history it is known that in April of 1814, Napoleon capitulated, and by arrangement with the allied Sovereigns was sent to the Island of Elba, and the career of the Emperor Napoleon was supposed to have been brought to an end. All the nations who had been engaged in the recent wars, and particularly our own, who had so largely participated in it, were beginning to rejoice at the return of peace. At this time our country held a high position, so much so that in June of that year, all the allied Sovereigns showed their high regard for England by coming to visit our Royal Family and people. And we gave them such an ovation as probably they never experienced before. Special arrangements had been made for the accommodation of the Emperor of Russia; a Palace at St. James's was splendidly fitted up for his reception, and for the Generals who accompanied him. Of the Prussians, Blucher was the most popular.

Having overheard that the allied Sovereigns had arranged to visit Ascot, I felt a great desire to go and see Blucher, but without permission I had no means of riding there. On the morning of Ascot Heath Races I arose at four, and having taken some food and a little money, I started on my way determined to see Blucher, and by eight o'clock I had arrived somewhere near Bracknell Turnpike. I was very tired, and seeing a neat little cottage with garden in front I ventured in and tapped at the door. 'Come in,' said someone; 'what may you please to want?' 'Will you be so good as to give me a glass of water?' I replied, 'as I am very thirsty.' 'If you will sit down I will get it you,' said a kindly spoken matronly looking woman; 'you look tired, maybe you have come from Wokingham?' 'I have walked from Reading.' I replied. 'Never! what this morning?' 'Yes,' I answered, 'and I am going to see Blucher.' She seemed amazed, and turned to fetch some water, but hesitated and said, 'Maybe you would like a little breakfast? I am just going to have mine; if

51

you don't mind my homely way, I can give you some new milk.' We sat down, and I made an excellent breakfast. In reply to my question, she said that her name was Sargent, that she was a widow, and had only one son, but he was gone to sea. 'I hope,' she added, 'that as he is very young, he will have enough of it in one voyage; I want him to learn a trade, for his father was a carpenter.' I was in the act of leaving when she said, 'You do look all the better for a good wash, but it is astonishing to me how any mother could let one so young go to the races; it is a bad place for men, and not a fit place for a young boy.' I replied that I had no mother. 'Poor lad!' she exclaimed, 'that is very *unked* for you; have you no father either?' 'Yes, I have, but I left him fast asleep; had he been awake I should not have been here.' With many thanks I left the good widow Sargent, who said she hoped that the Lord would take care of me, 'for very bad people went to the races sometimes.' Goodbye, widow Sargent; time has not robbed me of my sense of your kindness to a stranger. In after years, I had an opportunity of performing an act of kindness to her son, which widow Sargent did not live to thank me for.

I arrived at Ascot some time before the races were to commence, but even then there were several rows of carriages down the whole length of the course, and an immense mass of people. I walked to the bottom of it, where I saw Townsend, at the time a well-known Bow Street officer, giving instructions to his men, who were usually called Bow Street Runners; this was before we had the present order of Police. When the Royal party arrived the scene was wonderful and extremely grand. The Queen and Prince Regent were the first to arrive, and in quick succession all the Royal visitors and Generals who had taken part in the war which had so recently ended, but I do not remember to have seen the Duke of Wellington there; probably he was abroad with the residue of our army. Platow and Blucher arrived soon after Royalty, and the people gave them an enthusiastic reception, and tried to catch Blucher by the hand. When he and Platow left the Royal Stand they tried to get away on horseback, but the people ran after them cheering and wanting to shake hands, but their horses were alarmed, or the Generals tickled them with their spurs, and so got away. By this time I was used up, and began to seriously wonder how I was going to get home; by chance I saw Captain Montagu's carriage, and went to a man who played the key bugle, and told him that I wanted to hang on behind; this I eventually did without observation, but when we were going down the hill on this

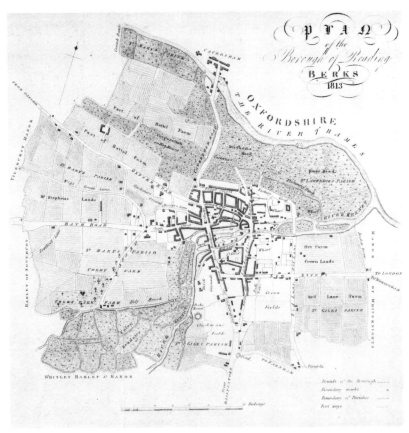

A map of Reading in 1813.

side of Wokingham I thought the four horses had bolted, and I was foolish enough to drop off behind. I rolled over and over cutting my face and hands very badly. Fortunately a gentleman was walking on the path (which was much above the level of the road), and he, with great presence of mind, pulled me up on to the path or I should certainly have been killed by the carriages and horsemen following us. I was partially stunned and bled a good deal. He very kindly took me to a small inn where there is a mill; 'Bob's Mill' it was then called; and the good matronly hostess washed my wounds, and gave me milk and bread and butter which the gentleman offered to pay for, but the good woman would not take anything. In this plight I started to walk home, which

53

was six miles distant, but at King Street I was met with our pony and chaise, and an angry parent, with whom I had to settle matters, having also the prospective view of another settlement at school. When I was chaffed by my playfellows for the thrashing I had given me, my reply was that I had seen Blucher and they had not.

In Reading there was great rejoicing. Bells were frequently ringing and flags were kept up for several days. There were public dinners, and the prisoners of war were ordered to their respective countries. Subscriptions were raised on their behalf, and I saw about sixty leave one morning, and as there were many Danes and Germans who had been living so long in the town they had many friends who regretted their departure. White cockades and sprigs of laurel (not primroses) were the order of the day.

I must here insert an amusing paragraph which appeared in the *Times* in the beginning of this year: 'The dragoon who was sent from London on Wednesday evening at six o'clock with the particulars of the Marquis of Wellington's victory did not arrive at Windsor till four o'clock in the morning, in consequence of losing his way in the fog, although he procured a candle and lanthorn from Hounslow, but which proved to be of no use to him.'

The following is 'Berkshire' literature of that year :- 'Bonaparte dethroned; the downfall of the most blasphemous beast that ever cursed the earth.' 'Heaven grant that the loyal population of France may break the chains prepared for them, and by ridding the earth of the Corsican murderer do their duty to Europe and mankind.' 'The first enormous blunder was in not hanging Napoleon when he was declared to be dethroned.'

A diminutive journeyman tailor of the name of Hilton, in the employ of Mr. Cottrill, of London Street, was dressed in the costume of Napoleon and rode a donkey through the streets, accompanied by a miscellaneous throng, some carrying loaves stuck on the top of short poles with 'cheap bread' written on the cards attached; this was the south end, or Silver Street, mode of rejoicing. On the 5th July there was a general illumination and some magnificent displays of appropriate devices. I remember a brilliant one at Madame Mistayer's in London

Street, 'Thank God,' in variegated lamps, and the Town Hall was a brilliant affair. There were several transparencies (painted very cleverly for so young a man) by the late Mr. Sims, the gilder, of London Street, the most attractive being that of Blucher.

I think it was on the 25th July, 1814 that we were aroused by the firing of cannon, I suppose in the Forbury. We were quickly in the street, but the indefatigable Dr. Golding was before us; this was the day for a public dinner to be held in the street, and the men in our employ had to be called out to erect some of the tables in London Street. When the whole was completed they extended from the Crown Inn, London Street, to the upper part of Friar Street. It was a fact, I believe, that there were 80 principal tables, each 40 feet long, 480 stewards appointed with carvers, and at a given signal 6,000 persons sat down to a splendid old English hot dinner. In the afternoon there were all sorts of sports in the Forbury, with bands of music; and the fair sex, with a corresponding proportion of our young townsmen, took possession of the new market and there danced until the early hours of the morning.

All things come to an end, and so did our rejoicings. Cheap bread we did not get, and John Bull had to pay the piper. Napoleon was now supposed to have been finally disposed of, and in Reading, as also in the county, public meetings were being held for the discussion of grievances. Our members, Messrs. Lefevre and Simeon, had a lively time of it, not only attending these meetings, but in presenting and supporting petitions for the remission of taxation. It seems to have escaped the notice of our fathers, that although the war was happily ended, the cost of it had to be provided for, and so it was that the sought-for relief was not realised. At this time the working classes were suffering great privations, as there was very little call for their services, and provisions of all kinds were very dear.

The effects of the recent war were speedily demonstrated by the return of many sick and wounded to Reading, some of whom had been held as prisoners of war in France for considerable periods. Besides these sufferers, we had many others here and in the county, who were partially or wholly blind from opthalmia caught in the earlier war in Egypt. Some of these invalids from the East could be easily distinguished from others on account of their wearing green shades or

55

coloured glasses. At the time to which I now refer, our late esteemed friend Mr. George May was getting into repute, and I believe that he had made the eye a subject for special study. He conceived the idea of establishing an Infirmary for these cases which were then so numerous. He very soon took a house in St. Mary's Butts, on the face of which was affixed a board, with a notice that diseases of the eye would be treated gratuitously during certain hours. Mr. May had the assistance of Dr. Greenhead, the Medical Officer to the Berkshire Militia, in this benevolent undertaking. As I am writing this merely from memory I refrain from venturing to name the year of this occurrence, but I am anxious to record a most interesting case which came under my own notice, and which does great honour to the memory of our late townsman, and did much, I think, to establish his reputation as a skilful surgeon.

After the war which induced our Government to send an army to Egypt, one of the men was invalided home suffering from opthalmia, and, according to his own account, was discharged from a hospital incurably blind. I remember him as residing in or about Reading for at least twenty years, always being led by his wife. In the rod-stripping season he was usually employed at Johnson's in Watlington Street, or at Twyford, at this occupation. For some years he and his wife lived in the Court opposite Simond's Bank in King Street; and one would think that there are many people living of middle-age who often saw him carrying water in pails with yokes from the Market Place pump. An interval occurred in which I lost sight of him, but on my driving down the Shepherd's House Hill one morning about the year 1838 I met a man on horseback cantering up the hill who so much resembled the blind man that I was in doubt whether or not it was he, but on reflection I came to the conclusion that the thing was impossible. I was not long in suspense, for a few days afterwards I met him in the King's Road carrying a bundle towards Reading, and he was alone. I stopped him and found that my conjecture was right. He stated that he had been discharged as incurable, but with a small pension; that he had been totally blind for so many years that he had no hope of ever seeing again, but with the little he could do and with the help of his wife they managed to live. 'Some ladies induced Mr. George May to see me, and after examination he said 'If you strictly follow my advice, I think it possible that your sight may be restored.' I had been blind so long that I thought that at all events he could do me no harm, so I placed myself under his care, and he performed an operation. The light was gradually admitted with the result which you see. I now go about without any difficulty, and am living at Twyford.'

Allusion to the above case induces me to mention that in the year 1813, and subsequently, I accompanied a relative to Windsor for the purpose of meeting the occulist who was attending His Majesty George the Third, and on these occasions I saw His Majesty walking on the terrace, accompanied by one of the gentlemen about Court. How wonderful it seems that I should have been blessed with health so that 73 years afterwards I had the honour of dining with the King's great grandson in Reading.

This autumn (1814) our Government made the sad mistake of reducing the strength of the army and navy. Some of the Blues, which regiment lay here under the command of Colonel Sir John Elly (at that time Major), were discharged, but before leaving the town they provided themselves with neckerchiefs at the 'Beehive,' draper's shop, opposite the Town Hall, and having removed the barbarous old-fashioned stiff leather stocks from their necks they threw them into the muddy road and played hockey with them. I think that these men, by their accent, came from Yorkshire.

Our Militia Regiments were in some cases disbanded, and the Berkshire, which was in Ireland, was ordered home. The officers in command were Col. Blagrave and the Adjt. Purvis. Two ships were provided, one an old steady-going vessel, into which a part of the Regiment embarked, and the other a new fast sailing one, in which the commanding officers with the band started; singularly enough the old vessel arrived in three days, but the new one was caught in a gale and did not land until the ninth day, when she put in at Liverpool. As may be imagined great anxiety was felt for her safety. This part of the Regiment was three weeks marching to Reading, but the former were stationed at Wokingham. A widow of the name of Joseph, who was in our service, had three sons, who were either 'drawn' or became substitutes, in the Berkshire Militia, two of whom were at Wokingham. An anecdote, which I think was pretty freely mentioned in reference to Col. Ravenshaw, and which I think did him honour, had reference to a young and very efficient officer in his Regiment, but who was not upon very cordial terms with his brother officers. The Colonel seems to have noticed this, and subsequently ascertained that the cause arose from the officer in question having relatives engaged in trade, and this fact induced them to 'cut' him. This state of things led the Colonel to pay marked attention to him, occasionally walking with him on parade before the men fell in, but he did not in like manner notice the other officers. This had had the desired effect, and afterwards the officers became friends.

— 5 —
Waterloo and After

Recollections of Reading veterans - a visit to the battlefield.

On or about the 18th March, 1815, I saw people in groups talking rather excitedly in London Street, and I soon found the cause; it was announced in the *Courier* paper that Napoleon had escaped from Elba and had landed at Antibes, in the South of France, and that he was marching on Lyons accompanied by some six thousand men; also that almost the whole French Army, which had sworn allegiance to Louis XVIII., had declared for the Emperor. In Reading there was great excitement, as many of our soldiers were at home on furlough; these were ordered to immediately join their regiments, and the drum and fife were once more heard in our streets, where nine months before a public dinner was held to commemorate peace. Wellington, I believe, had not returned to England, but was sent for to go immediately to Belgium. A month afterwards I was awoke about four o'clock in the morning by the sound of music. I immediately arose and opened the window looking into London Street. On the east side there was a long line of men, some of them in regimentals, others partially so, and very many recruits with their friends. They marched three abreast, and were accompanied by a musician at their head, who played the 'British Grenadier' very nicely on a violin, and at that early hour it had a cheering effect. These men, I was informed, were marching to their respective regiments or depots. Birch, of the Blues, was here on furlough, and had been married only a month; orders came for him to immediately join his regiment. Orders also arrived that the men of the 7th Hussars should join their regiment, which, I believe, was at Hounslow. Volunteering from the Berkshire Militia was resorted to, and two out of three sons of the widow who was in our service volunteered and fought at Waterloo; one was wounded but both returned home again. It seems that there was not sufficient time to clothe the Volunteer Militia then, for some 20 years after the engagement I saw a Berkshire Militia jacket hanging up in the museum at Waterloo, which, I was informed by Sergeant-Major Cotton, was worn by one of our men who fell there. To revert again to April, 1815, on my return from Oakingham, I saw a group of persons at the lower end of Silver Street, amongst whom was a Reading man of the name of Lyons. He had been taken prisoner by the French in Spain, but was liberated on the occasion of Napoleon being sent to Elba. He was busily engaged in obtaining some young men to join the army, and he, with Sergeant York and others, had induced John Somerset (a fine young fellow) to enlist in the 7th Hussars, and Lyons was teaching his recruit (who, by-the-bye, was rather unsteady) the sword exercise. I believe that others enlisted in the 7th with Somerset. He was soon sent to join the regiment, but he could not have had more than two months' drill. He was in the charge on the 17th June, and was wounded with a Lancer's spear in the neck and a shot through his hand. He fell into the hands of the French, but was released on the 18th June, and was soon in Reading again. Somerset had a pension of a shilling a day until his death, which probably did not occur until fifty years after the battle. He must be remembered by many, as he lived close to Wheeler's carriage works in Mill Lane, and was always a javelin man at the Assizes. When I visited Waterloo for the first time, Sergeant-Major Cotton was the guide, and in alluding to the 7th Hussars, of which he was a member, he described the charge of the French Lancers as 'fatal to forty of our men who were killed outright in consequence of the English horses becoming frightened at the fluttering of the small flags attached to the lances, which, when the men were within three or four horses' lengths, were suddenly lowered; this caused the English horses to swerve, and thus the loss on our side. Lord Paget led the Light Cavalry, but they were withdrawn after this charge, and it was in this affair that Somerset came to grief. Lord Paget subsequently placed himself at the head of the Blues and Life Guards, with whom he charged the French Lancers and literally rode them down.' Upon the second occasion of my visiting Waterloo, about 25 years since, Sergeant-Major Cotton was lying in a tomb in the orchard of Hugomont, where he at his own request was buried. His niece, whom he had brought up from her infancy, was married to a Belgian, and they had the care of the Museum in which are kept relics of the contest. She became much interested at my mentioning the names of some of our Reading men, whom I had seen enlisted. She made the remark that her uncle said that Reading had almost furnished a troop for the 7th.

On my first visit to Waterloo Sergt.-Major Cotton took me and my friends into the orchard at Hugomont, and gave a very interesting account of the struggle between the French and English for the possession of this place. It was held by the Coldstream Guards, it being the key of our position. The orchard was enclosed with a brick wall which the Duke had loopholed. There was a small chapel near the farm in which hung a wooden crucifix. This caught fire during the battle, and the lower part of it was burnt. At the time of my visit the walls of the chapel were covered with autographs, written with pencil; amongst them I could decipher the names of Byron, Shelley and other well-known Englishmen. At the village of Waterloo there was exhibited in a glass case the wreck of a boot worn by the Marquess of Anglesea, whose foot was hit by a cannon shot. In the adjoining burying ground there was a monument recording this event, under which I was told the said foot was interred with the arm of Lord Fitzroy Somerset, which was amputated in a house opposite. In the little chapel were tablets on the walls erected by loving parents or friends in memory of some very juvenile officers who fell in this deadly struggle. I remember two brothers named Joshua and Caleb Hawkins, whose parents resided in St. Giles' parish. The former belonged to the 7th Hussars and was with his regiment at the Battle of Corunna. Joshua Hawkins informed me that on the whole of the Christmas Day (1808-9) he was picketed with his Regiment on the heights watching the movements of the French under Marshall Soult, and they were without food the whole time. At night-fall they were ordered to retire and follow the main army which had already commenced their retreat on Corunna. On arriving at a small town some of the men rode into an inn yard and asked for refreshments, but the master of the hotel said they had nothing for themselves; three of the four fellows dismounted and entered the inn with drawn swords and soon found some loaves secreted in a corn bin; these they appropriated, but by this time a crowd had assembled, and some stones were thrown at them. Hawkins and his companion were soon in their saddles again and they had to charge the mob before they could get away; and these were the people, he remarked, whom we came to rescue from their French oppressors and who had promised our Government to assist them with an Army. The Battle of Corunna and the death of Sir John Moore followed. At the close of the Peninsula campaign, Hawkins left the Army, and came to Reading, his native place. Here he became a market gardener and eventually built himself a cottage on his own land. For fifty years this good man held meetings at his home for scripture reading, and many are at this time living who can testify to the good this brave English soldier did in the immediate neighbourhood of Waterloo Road and Spring Gardens.

Caleb Hawkins was Sergeant in the 14th Light Dragoons, and was at Waterloo. A short time after the engagement he wrote to his sister (Mrs. Raggett, of London Street) such an interesting account of the battle that it was publicly read from the steps of the Post Office in London Street, and those assembled to hear it gave three ringing cheers for the British Army.

Mr. Moody, proprietor of the one o'clock coach, brought the earliest official report of the engagement, which he read aloud from the same spot, and the report wound up by stating that the Blues suffered severely.

I am reminded that in referring to the number of Reading men who were in this engagement, I omitted to mention the name of Williams; he enlisted in the waggon train, and had risen to be sergeant. During the battle he was engaged with the ambulance in bringing away the wounded. On one occasion, as he was leaving with some badly wounded officers, he heard a faint cry for water from a young officer who had been severely wounded. Williams gave him not only water, but some brandy from his own flask. He and his comrades lifted him into their waggon and brought him safely to Brussels. On their arrival he was promptly attended to, and recovered sufficiently to ask Williams to take charge of a locket which he wore, and also his watch 'for,' said he, 'I fear I shall not recover, but should you be fortunate enough to return home, which is very probable, as the battle, I think, is won and the enemy in full retreat, let me beg of you to call and leave these things at the War Office and make known my name. If I survive you shall hear from me.' This young officer did recover, and on reaching England went to the War Office, where he found his watch and the more valuable (to him) locket. When Williams returned home he was rewarded with a gift of forty pounds, and on leaving the service he received a pension of either 2s. 6d. or 3s. 6d. per day for life.

After the war was brought to a close, one of the Blues by the name of

A view of Southampton Street, known in Darter's youth as Horn Street.

Mallard returned to Reading and became a riding-master. He and his wife had the care of the late Dr. Hooper's baths. Mallard informed me that at Waterloo his regiment was in a corn field, and both men and horses were getting some food, when a gentleman on horseback, who had ridden over from Brussels, gave them notice that a strong force of the enemy's cavalry could be seen coming down towards them. He said: 'We were quickly in our saddles, and, having formed with the Life Guards, we were led by Lord Paget, and our fellows 'knocked over the lot.' ' In this affair the Lancers who had so recently inflicted severe loss on the 7th Hussars were literally ridden down. In this charge Major Pack was killed, and Colonel Sir John Elly wounded; both these officers were in Reading with their regiment not long before the engagement. In conversing with Mallard's wife at the Baths, she gave me an account of the great anxiety she and another woman (whose husband was in Mallard's troop) felt, and the trials they had gone through in getting to Brussels. While there, and during the three days' fighting, constant reports of disaster to the English were brought by some of the Belgian allies, who had bolted from the conflict at the smell of powder. These women managed to make their way by getting into the wood of Soignies, which runs parallel with the road to Waterloo. On their way they heard that the Blues were in the hottest of the fight, and they determined at all hazards to go over the battle field in search of their husbands, who they apprehended slain. Having learnt, through the information given them by the ambulance people, where the Blues were mostly engaged, they soon found a great many of the dead, and while turning over some of the bodies they obtained information that their husbands were safe and on their march to Paris; this proved to be true. Mallard had a pension, and for several years I signed his pension paper for him, but the last time I did so his memory had entirely failed him.

Late in the autumn of 1815 I was returning from London with my father inside Williams' coach, and there were with us an English officer and Mr. Wakefield, a barrister, living at Hare Hatch. The conversation related principally to the late battle, in which this officer had been engaged. Some of the details were distressingly painful to hear, and he stated that he with his regiment had been employed in collecting the dead and burning them, and that 'when the flames reached a good fat fellow he burned like a tar barrel.' This officer made so light of this horrid affair that he was soon down to zero in my boyish estimation.

Waterloo was for some time a favourite name for streets, roads and buildings. William Williams, the proprietor of the Reading coach, occupied at this time a farm at Whitley, and he gave it the name of Waterloo Farm, and the road leading to it Waterloo Road.

Some time after the end of the war, Napoleon's carriage was, with four horses, driven down London Street by the coachman who was with his master at Waterloo, and also his valet, the latter having lost an arm. The carriage and internal fittings were exhibited in the Forbury for several days, and were full of interest.

This train of thought induces me to mention the name of a gallant officer long resident amongst us, whom I should be sorry to omit, as it is associated with military events in which the above-mentioned men were engaged: I allude to the late Captain Purvis, whose name reminds me of a trifling anecdote. From the year 1821 until 1830 I was a member of a troop of Yeomanry which was originally raised by Lord Sidmouth, who gave it the name of the Woodley Troop, and it was subsequently commanded by Captain Montague. In the year 1826, about the middle of May, all the Regiments of Berkshire Yeomanry assembled at Newbury on 'permanent duty,' and were reviewed on Greenham Common by a General Officer sent from the War Office. We returned to Reading on the 29th May, and our annual dinner took place immediately afterwards. Captain Purvis at that time was Adjutant in the Berkshire Militia, and was invited to dine with us. In the course of the evening Captain Fuller Craven, who commanded the Vale of White Horse Troop, proposed Purvis' health, and stated that he had a narrow escape at Corunna, as the French put a shot through his (Purvis') cap.

I feel that I cannot part with Captain Purvis without saying that he was one of the most genial men it has ever been my good fortune to meet, and at the time of his decease he was our senior magistrate. After the Captain retired from the regular Army, which I presume to have occurred about the year 1814, he married, and for a time lived at Whitley. In 1822 he occupied Watlington House, and during the incumbency of the Rev. F. Trench, who built St. John's Church, he became Churchwarden to him, and subsequently to the present esteemed vicar, the Rev. Canon Payne; it was at Watlington House that the Captain ended his useful life. About the year 1814, Captain Purvis was with the Berks Militia, then lying in Ireland, and when the Regiment came home in 1815 it was finally stationed at Reading. After the conclusion of the war the regiment was disembodied and the band broken up, excepting what was called the drum and fife band and the staff, which were retained, and were actively engaged whenever the Militia was called out. On ordinary occasions, both staff and band were drilled either in the Forbury or in a meadow adjacent to Captain Purvis' residence., by an excellent non-commissioned officer, Sergeant-Major Preston. The drum and fife band was one of the best for its number that I have ever heard, and it was a great treat to go to the Forbury on a Sunday morning in those days and see the staff march to St. Lawrence's Church, with the band at their head, playing, 'Hark, the Bonnie Christ Church Bells,' and after the service return marching to a quick step. My memory dwells on the whole scene as it was at that period, before modern requirements interfered with the neighbourhood and intercepted from our view some of the beautiful scenery in Oxfordshire. To revert again to the band, there were some excellent musicians in it, some of whom will be even now remembered, for instance, the two brothers of the name of Kates, the elder of whom is mentioned in Mr. Binfield's programme of the musical festival in the year 1819. I must not omit to mention the name of Penny; he was the very best player on the small drum that I ever heard, and although the mention of this would seem too trivial to be worth recording (excepting to Reading men), I have seen little groups of people, and amongst them soldiers of other regiments wait in London Street to hear him beat the usual *reveille* (or roll call). The music for this small band was arranged by the late master, Mr. Smith, who was with the Berkshire Militia in Ireland; it was unique of its kind, being before keys were applied to bugles, French horns, &c., the half tones being produced by inserting a hand into the bell of the instrument. The music in question was arranged for flutes with a tenor drum (which was tuned) and beaten by a smart fellow of the name of Cray; also a large drum, and a novel accompaniment for first and second bugles, played respectively by Edward Blagrave and George Adams, and what they had to do was most effective.

All the men to whom I refer have passed away, with the exception of one; he is, I believe, about 83 years of age, and was a boy on board the transport ship which brought part of the regiment from Ireland, and was eight days making the passage to Liverpool. All the men in both band and staff were, with few exceptions, natives of Reading, and in the prime of life, but, to quote an old ballad, 'They will never march again.'

— 6 —
Sports

Sports in the Forbury - bull baiting at Wokingham - prize fighting at Ruscombe - revels at Woodley and Peppard - river bathing.

In the year 1809 I was taken to the Forbury to see the sports which were to be held there to commemorate the 50th year of the reign of George the Third. The sports consisted of donkey racing, climbing greasy poles, (at the top of which were affixed prizes of different sorts), and also other games usually seen at fairs. The most amusing incident in these amusements which is impressed on the memory of my childhood occurred in the attempts to get at the prizes on the top of the greasy poles, and particularly one which was the most valuable, viz., a leg of mutton with a bunch of ribbons attached. Several attempts were made, both by men and boys, but they invariably failed. As, however, they brought away a portion of grease, each successor got higher. When most of them had given it up, a smart young sailor, who was come from his ship to see his parents, and who had been quietly looking on, made an attempt, and when he reached a higher point than the others, Jack found his troubles begin, at least it was thought so. The people cheered him lustily, and he very pluckily worked away, now and again putting his hand in his side pockets for something which turned out to be coarse sand, but at the time the onlookers did not know that. The cheering continued as he slowly ascended; at last Jack clutched his prize and came down like a shot. There was a rush to the spot, people thinking our hero was hurt, but he was, he said, all right.

About the year 1815, one of our leading tradesmen asked my father if he would allow me to drive him in our pony chaise as far as King Street, which is about five miles on the Wokingham Road. To this he assented, and on arrival there my friend drew my attention to the number of people on their way towards Wokingham, and suggested the we might

Dr. Valpy's Reading School with boys playing in the Forbury.

as well go and see what was going on there. This suggestion I readily acquiesced in, and we drove to the Inn in the Market Place, which commanded a view of the Bull Baiting, of which I previously had no knowledge, but my friend must have planned the whole thing, for after placing me at a front first-floor window he went away for a time and returned with a Mr. Norris, who had, as I discovered from their conversation, arranged to meet him there. It was St. Thomas' Day, which was dark, damp and foggy. There was a great and miscellaneous concourse, including some soldiers from Windsor and a number of the Blues from Reading. Very soon a stir occurred amongst the people, and they ran in all directions out of the way of a fine young bull, which was on his way towards the Market Place. When the animal arrived he was fixed to a ring which was attached to an oak post level with the ground. The bull had about five yards of chain, and at first dashed about and tried to get his liberty; this had the effect of making the people rush against each other, and many of them tumbled down in the mud. Soon arose a cry of 'A lane, a lane'; this was for the people to form a narrow avenue leading up to the bull, which was quickly done, in deference, I presume, to some authority, and then a man holding a bull-dog between his knees would let him slip and run up the 'lane' to catch hold of the bull's nose, which, if he succeeded, would pin his head down, and this would be called 'pinning the bull.' In this case, the dog, which I heard was brought from Staines, ran at the animal who instantly caught him on his horns and threw him high in the air. The people immediately closed together to catch him, or probably his neck would have been broken. A man named Baker, of Reading, whom we passed on the road in the morning, a smart young fellow, wearing a clean white smock frock, was one of those who assisted in catching this dog. The poor thing was bleeding, and as he fell one of his legs caught Baker's nose and lip which were set bleeding, and I never saw such an altered picture in so short a time, for he was bespattered with mud and blood so that no one could have believed it to be the same person. Another dog, a small one, next set on the bull, and during the day there was not one of the many dogs which so nearly succeeded as this courageous little fellow. I think the owner of it obtained a prize for his little black dog. I did not see one of them successful. Another dog ran under the bull and punished him so by fixing on a tender part that in its agony it broke chain and ran down the street. It was some time before they brought him back, and then it was supposed that he had been baited enough, for he was taken to the slaughterhouse and immediately killed. Another, a smaller bull, was then brought out and similarly baited. By this time, the light, which had been very imperfect, became worse, so that I could not see quite the end, but I was informed that one of the dogs had been thrown on to the low roof of an old Market House. Then the men, most of whom had been quarrelling, took to fighting, and almost the whole of the mob were much in the same state as Baker, to whom I have alluded. Taking the affair altogether, a more brutalising scene could not well be concieved. I was indebted for this elevating spectacle to a gentleman whose name I forbear to mention, as I should be sorry to wound the susceptibilities of his descendants, who of late years have been struggling to get into a higher sphere and mix with the 'upper ten thousand,' but at present they are similar in a position to Mahomet's coffin, and there I leave them.

Having already alluded to the cruelty of bull baiting, as practised in this country, I will describe what I know of prize fighting. My apology for doing so is the example of Charles Dickens, who, that he might be instrumental in abolishing public executions, remained all night near Newgate and mixed with the crowd who had assembled to witness the execution of Manning and his wife for murder. His account of the scene and the conduct of those who had assembled there was no doubt the primary cause of the abolition of public executions, and I should be thankful, indeed, if I could in the most trifling degree assist in suppressing such scenes as I propose to describe. I fear, however, that there is a tendency to revive prize fighting, for a few weeks since a contest of this kind occurred not very far from us, and although it lasted over an hour, no one interfered to stop it. It is nearly sixty years since that I, with a friend, was driving through Twyford on our way to keep an appointment at Knowl Hill, but seeing several carriages and many persons on foot going towards Ruscombe Lake, which is near Twyford, we found on inquiry that they were on their way to see a prize fight between two celebrated Boxers. Up to that moment neither of us had any idea that a contest of this kind was about to occur. The place chosen was near Ruscombe Church, and not a mile, I should think, from Twyford. As we were leaving the latter place, a gentlemanly looking person asked us if we would kindly allow his friend (who was a professional man) to ride with us, and as his friend looked as he was described, we did not hesitate to oblige him. When we arrived at a meadow we saw that a roped ring had been formed. Here we were stopped at the gate, and obliged to pay a shilling for admission. The 'professional gentleman' here alighted, and thanked us 'for giving him a lift.' In wishing us good morning he said 'I am going to fight Josh Hudson's Black.'

When we arrived at the ring, we found it surrounded with four-horse breaks and vehicles of all sorts, besides a great number of people. Before the fight began I saw a few of the aristocracy inside the ring (talking to friends of the combatants), one of them, a neighbouring baronet, with whose name we are all familiar even now, and there were also many others of similar social position. Inside the ropes were the bottle holders and seconds, also celebrated pugilists. Peter Crawley and the celebrated light weight, Dick Curtis, seconded one of the name of 'Whiteheaded Bob,' who, when he entered the ring, was a perfect picture of a man. He was dressed in white flannel, had white curly hair, and when he stripped down to the waist he appeared as fair in complexion as any man I ever saw, and there did not seem to be a blemish about him. Then came 'Jem Burns,' a taller man, but not so well built as his opponent. As soon as he was stripped the men were placed in the position assigned them, but I do not remember which of them 'won the toss.' They then shook hands and began sparring, but some time elapsed before a blow was struck. At last Burns hit his man straight in the face, which knocked him against the ropes, and he fell before Burns could inflict another blow. Several rounds followed of a similar character, and it seem that Burns must win on account of his being longer in the reach. If I mistake not, the latter, by hitting Bob on the head, injured his hand, as his seconds poured cold water on it, and threw water on his face. The next round Bob, after receiving two or three severe hits, by indomitable pluck got into close quarters, and then ensued a most fearful struggle; Bob's head was 'in chancery,' but he pommelled away at Burns' ribs with his right hand, and the latter punished Bob's face; so they held together, the latter having his left arm round Burns' waist, and in this way fell against the ropes, both dreadfully punished by their backs being so badly cut. When again they were placed on the second's knees, they required much attention, for both were nearly exhausted, and Bob's face much disfigured.

By this time they had fought fully an hour. A few more rounds occurred, both men falling, the under one putting up his knees for protection, and the other falling so that he might injure his opponent. The next round was severely contested for men so weakened, and Burns knocked Bob off his legs (and some thought the battle over). At this moment an uncle of Burns pulled down the colours and claimed a win for his nephew, saying 'you will be tried for manslaughter if you go on.' The seconds, however, raised their men, who stood like dummies for a moment, not having power to raise thier arms; Dick Curtis at this moment called out loudly in his man's ear 'Bob, Bob.' The poor fellow looked up as if in a dream, and then bored his head against Burns; both fell at the ropes unable to move. They were instantly raised and restoratives given, but Burns made no response. When time was called Curtis and Crawley stuck up their man, but Burns was carried off the ground, and White-headed Bob was proclaimed victor.

I never before or since witnessed such wonderful courage as these men displayed, for, independent of the severe punishment they inflicted on each other, they were very much injured when coming in contact with the ropes. Several times during the fight Bob, when driven near them, would run back, and this gave him (by the spring of the rope) a quick forward movement, or he would have been sadly punished. When he was taken away his face and head presented a fearful spectacle; every feature was literally knocked out of him, and the wonder to my mind was how he, after such a fearful loss of blood, was able to sustain this protracted fight, for I think it continued for more than an hour-and-a-half. I was informed that the winner obtained a purse of 200 guineas, also that this sum was raised by subscription amongst the aristocracy, some of whom posted down from London to witness the fight.

A Mr. Basing, from Reading, had his watch stolen during the contest, and as he was mentioning the matter to me, a well-dressed man came up and said 'Have you lost anything, sir?' 'Yes,' said the man, 'My watch.' 'Would you like to have it again,' said the man, 'If so, what will you give, and I will see if I can get it for you?' 'Five pounds,' grumbled out my venerable friend. The man left us for a few minutes and then returned with the watch, but I could see that if any attempt had been made to seize it there were confederates near who would have attacked us.

It was clear to my mind that the magistrates and the police connived at this prize fight, for the battle occurred in a meadow belonging to one in authority. I had enough of this battle without waiting to see the 'professional gentleman's' performance. I never heard that he who was successful in this fight with Burns ever fought afterwards, but my impression is that he died within a year. Altogether, it was a most demoralising and shocking sight to see two men in the prime of life, who had no ill-feeling towards each other, fighting to the death for a purse of money, and for the gratification of those who subscribed the amount.

It is a singular fact, I believe, that prize fighting was not practised by other nations, although wrestling was; and as our fathers lived at a period of our history when we had nearly the whole of the world against us, it is probable that these trials of courage and endurance were universally practised by our people that we might the better be able to protect our shores. In this way, the youth of England became familiar with what we should now designate as brutal sports. I, myself, when a mere lad, remained on Ascot Heath after the racing to witness a prize fight which occurred opposite the Grand Stand. The gentlemen who remained on this stand subscribed a handsome sum, which induced two men to fight for their amusement. This sort of thing occurred on the last day of the races for many years.

To come nearer home, I venture to describe a revel which I saw at the Chequers Inn, at Woodley, and this was not the only one I witnessed there. About the year 1812, I was staying with an old servant of ours by the name of Leach, living near the Chequers, whose husband took me to see the Whitsuntide sports on 'Bunny Sheath,' as the illiterate called Bulmershe Heath. I soon had enough of it, for I saw a fellow's head cut, and blood flow. At this I showed the 'white feather,' and retired, while the people shouted a chorus of 'A head, a head,' with clapping of hands.

A year or two after this, I was taught single stick with other boys, and we had basket handles to our weapons. Whether this amusement gave me more confidence than in past days I cannot say, but, at all events, I found my way to the Woodley revels a year or two later, and did not require a guide. It was Whitsuntide, and fine weather. There was a large and miscellaneous assembly. Gipsies and fortune tellers, gentlemen in carriages, farmers in traps, besides horsemen, surrounded a roped ring of about twelve yards' diameter. I was sitting on a chaise, and had a good view of the game. Someone threw his hat into the ring, and shortly after another did the same in answer to the challenge, and the two men having divested themselves of all superfluous clothing, and being supplied by the referee with cudgels with basket handles, they began fencing. One of them received a blow on the head which drew blood, and there was a general shout of 'A head.'

Two other men then began to play, and one of them having hit his opponent unfairly, there was a cry of 'foul blow.' The combatants threw down their sticks and began fighting; the ring was broken into, and a general row ensured; so, like many others, I escaped to a place of safety.

In 1816 I patronised these sports again, and I thought the whole thing more quietly managed. Amongst the players was a man by the name of

Cue, a sawyer, who was considered a first-rate hand; he took a 'head,' as it was called, but by brutal violence, and some of the people called out 'Shame.' A man from Reading, who was very well known as a carman, by the name of Fuller, became the next antagonist to Cue. No sooner did they begin to fence than Cue struck Fuller a violent blow on his left arm, which nearly broke it; this evidently excited the audience against Cue. Fuller had his arm bound and continued the contest in great agony. He having left, Cue, who seemed elated at his success, was met by a challenge made by a young, smartly-dressed man of about 25 years of age, who wore a light blue smock frock, and who was recognised as a calfman from Wantage. He was very quiet in his manner, and seemed self-possessed and deliberate. As soon as Cue faced the calfman he began his old game, by staring his antagonist in the face, at the same moment making a violent blow at his left arm. This was very dexterously parried, and Cue received a touch on the head, which was applauded. Cue, being foiled in his attempts, seemed to lose heart, for he made desperate attempts to get at his opponent's head by striking at his arm or shoulder, which were very cleverly parried, and Cue shortly after got his head broken, to the great satisfaction of a large gathering. This was my last appearance at a revel.

The revels at Woodley, and also the races, were not held at Bulmershe Heath since about 72 years ago, at which period the Mr. Wheble of that date enclosed the common and planted it. He, however permitted the South Berks Yeomanry to drill there, and allowed cricket matches to take place on the Heath.

It is now about 62 years since the Ruscombe Lake prize fight occurred and it will give a more perfect idea of the national feeling in reference to these exhibitions if I mention that at the pugilistic contests before mentioned, I saw, besides the Baronet, a curate, and the doctor of a neighbouring parish enjoying these sports; the former was so enamoured with the use of the gloves, and having more muscular power and money than zeal for his profession, used to invite a prize-fighter from London (who gave lessons in the noble art of self-defence) to come into the county and stay with him. Both the doctor and the curate lived within two miles of Twyford.

I quote from a printed report, headed, 'Peppard, Henley-on-

Thames,' March the 20th, 1880, as follows: 'The anniversary, always held on Whit-Monday, is perhaps the most popular village anniversary in England; its origin has no small interest connected with it; from time immemorial a most demoralizing revel had been held in the village every Whit-Monday; vast concourses assembled; drinking, fighting, brutalising sports, and the most awful immorality characterised the scene. Suffice it to say the vile revel has at length become extinct.'

Towards the close of the last century and the early part of this, revels at Whitsuntide were common amongst us, and they had a brutalising effect upon our people. Our sanguinary laws then in force only aggravated the evil by making men familiar with deeds of violence and reckless of human life. It is not improbable that the murder of William Bellimore, the Mortimer carrier, by two youths named Abraham Tull and William Hawkins, was suggested to their minds by being accustomed to witness these revels, and I don't think that the execution of these young fellows by hanging them in chains on Mortimer Common and leaving them until their bones fell out of their gibbets had any deterring effect. In connection with this dismal story, I may mention that about 50 years ago the late Rev. Mr. Hodgkinson came into Mr. Lovejoy's Library at the moment that I was stating that I had that day seen the weapon with which this crime was committed, as also the watch which was taken from the murdered man. The rev. gentleman was much interested, 'for,' said he, 'I gave religious instruction to the prisoners and accompanied them to their execution.' As the rev. gentleman expressed a desire to see the things I have mentioned, I referred him to a Mr. Truss, broker (long since deceased), London-street, who had shown them to me. Another event connected with this subject occurred a few weeks since when I entered our Museum. Dr. Stevens had just received some relics which refer to the above subject, and he was arranging them in a glass case, when I caught sight of a hand-bill, which I said I had seen before. It was, I added, shown me by the late Mrs. Spencer, of Mortimer, in the year 1820; it is the 'last dying speech,' &c., 'I know by its form and the stains on the paper.' Dr. Stevens confirmed that he had just received it from Mortimer.

I think it is very likely that for ages there were good places for bathing in Reading, and in the days of my boyhood the most popular with us youngsters were the Swing Bridge (the approach to which was

75

by Blake's Wharf); the 'Little Corner,' situate about half-way between the playground at Dr. Valpy's and the Lock Pool in the King's Meadows; and, for more expert swimmers, a place about a hundred yards beyond the Pound Keeper's house. I myself learnt to swim at 'Little Corner,' and it was quite safe, there being no holes and the depth not exceeding 3ft. 6in. or 4ft. Beyond it, and near the said lock, there was about 12 or 14 feet of water, and those who were good swimmers preferred this latter place. At the time to which I refer there was always a good current of water running through these spots, and it was navigable up to the foot of the incline from the Forbury; at this point there was a building called the granary, into which was sometimes stored either corn or flour belonging to Mr. Tubb, of Caversham Mill. When I last saw 'Little Corner' it had been spoiled for bathing, the bank having been trodden down and the water-course narrowed. Until the new bathing house was erected there was no safe place for young people to acquire the art of swimming. During my boyhood the King's Meadow was held by Mr. Jonathan Tanner, brewer, Castle Street. He was one of the few I remember to have worn powdered hair with pigtail, and also Hessian boots. He was much respected by a large circle of friends (one of whom was Dr. Widows Golding), and was a gentleman of imposing appearance. A medical student of the Doctor's, a Mr. Brooks, who I remember about the years 1815-16, took the pratice at the time Dr. Golding retired to a London practice. Dr. Golding built for himself a house just beyond Coley Avenue, and by occupying it before the walls were dry caught a chill which killed him. He was a warm supporter of the Literary Institution when Martin Annesley was Chairman.

For many years the King's Meadows continued in the occupation of Mr. Tanner, and during the summer months he and his two sons frequently rode down the towing path on horseback, particularly during hay harvest. At this season the bathers were a great nuisance, as they ran amongst the hay and threw it at each other after it was put together. This sport became pretty general when Mr. Tanner and his sons were near the swing bridge, which was the opposite side of the meadows, and whither they had gone to suppress a similar pastime. Then he and his sons would gallop across the meadow to catch the 'young rascals' near the pound, but in this they were baffled, for the 'look out' gave notice of their approach, and the boys pitched into the

Thames and mixed with those who had not trespassed. At last, Mr. Tanner determined that a stop should be put to this kind of amusement, and he caused several cart loads of broken bottles to be thrown into the deep water where the older boys bathed at the foot of the lock. This did not wholly prevent the bathing, but many persons were injured by having their feet cut, and ever afterwards this gentleman had the questionable honour of being dubbed Mr. Bottle Tanner.

Until very recently Reading, with an approximate population of 27,000 inhabitants, had no baths where ladies could learn the art of swimming, and it is entirely owing to the enterprising spirit of Mr. W.H. Simonds, builder, of South Street, that this necessity has been provided. I am sure he has the hearty good wishes of us all that it may prove a success. If it were not that the Corporation, as a Sanitary Authority, have already too much business on hand, I, for one, should have thought it was the duty of such a body to provide an establishment of this kind, especially as they have not only control over the supply of water, but the price to be paid for it.

I should not have alluded to the following personal incident but for the singular sequel. The part of the river into which the bottles were thrown was upon one occasion nearly fatal to me. About sixty-three years since I was passing through the Forbury with two sons of a relative on their way home, and when near the gaol we heard loud screams from the direction of the lock and clappers. It was a cold, dark night in February and on Sunday. Our impression was that a bargeman was ill-using a boy on board one of the boats, and as the cries for help were continuous, we made the best of our way towards the Thames, by keeping close to the wall, and after passing into the meadow it was not without considerable risk that we traced our way by keeping as close to the water as we could, the reflected light from the ripples assisting us. The cries were becoming more faint and spasmodic in consequence of the flushes of water (as we afterwards found) getting into the mouth of the person. On arriving at the spot we could see the head of a woman just above the water, but nearer to the opposite bank than to us. As soon as possible I threw off my coat and hat and plunged into the river, thinking that the person was standing, but I was quickly undeceived, and it was too dark to know exactly where I was. I, however, thought that the water could not be very deep, but to my surprise I discovered that I could not touch the bottom. I, however, swam to the person, and as soon as I reached her she caught hold of my arm and held me as if I were in a vice. I felt for the bottom of the river but could not reach it, and then it occurred to me to tear myself away, for what with the cold, the terror occasioned by her incessant screams, and the noise of rushing water, I became alarmed for my own safety. I, therefore, tried to release myself from her grasp, and in doing so kicked against a pile which was below the water (a foot, I think), for it could not be seen even the next morning. I immediately placed both feet against the post or pile, and by main force pulled away from it. At this moment her shrieks were distinctly heard in the Market Place, and many people came down, particularly some assistants from Mr. Hoskins, the linen draper. By keeping her at arms' length I managed to get her to the bank, where the people assisted us out. It was then noticed that the young woman had a pocket hankerchief tied to one arm, but she was too exhausted to speak beyond saying that she lived at the Pound House, and that her name was Ward. This was within a hundred yards of her home, and yet from the noise of the rushing water her father did not hear her cries. Having seen the poor girl taken to her home, I ran with my two companions to their house, which was about a quarter of a mile distant, where I was immediately placed between blankets, and with the assistance of a little stimulant I soon recovered from the shivering which the cold occasioned. The following morning I visited the girl who I found wrapped up and sitting by a good fire; Dr. Valpy being there and endeavouring to ascertain the particulars; but whether she had lost her voice from exercising her lungs so freely, or whether she feigned inability I cannot say for she replied in monosyllables and in a whisper. I told the doctor what I knew of the case, and mentioned that a hankerchief was found attached to her wrist. I ought to have stated that Dr. Valpy used to preach annually a sermon in aid of the funds of the Humane Society, therefore he always took great interest in cases of this sort.

Having recovered some things which I had lost the previous night, I went with others to examine more particularly the spot where this event happend. The conclusion we came to was that probably at a remote period a boat house or shed must have existed there, and that one of the ancient piles in the bed of the river had not been removed, but could be seen; also that the water near it varied in depth from 10 to 14 feet.

— 7 —
Music

Musical Societies and concerts - ringing in the New Year.

Early in the present century the late Mr. Binfield was the principal music master, there being only one other, Mr. Tanner, who, although a sound musician and excellent timeist, did not excel as an instrumentalist. At the earliest period of my memory Mr. Packer established a business in Mister Street as a watch-maker and jeweller, with whom was Mr. Trendell, who subsequently had this business in consequence of Mr. Packer's decease. The latter was succeeded by the late Mr. Bracher, now Messrs. Bracher and Sydenham. The Mr. Packer above referred to had a son who was educated as a musician and eventually became an organist at St. Mary's Church. About the year 1815 he had a music shop in Minster Street, the front pilasters of which were adorned with gilt organ pipes. Mr. Packer subsequently removed to a house in Castle Street and had a considerable amount of patronage as a teacher. This gentleman used to have an annual concert, at which most of the popular artistes of the day were engaged, supplemented by local amateurs. One of these was Mr. Richardson, who was also a dancing master with an extensive practice, but somehow Mr. Packer became annoyed at the interference of Mr. Richardson who, it seemed, always promoted Mr. Binfield's interest. This induced Mr. Packer to persuade Mr. Venua to come to Reading to teach dancing, and as this gentleman had been leader of the Ballette at the London Opera House, it was not a bad advertisement for him. This beginning of discord amongst the avowed promoters of harmony never ceased.

I think the period to which I am referring was about 1814 or 1815. Mr. Venua, who was a thorough musician and an able leader, felt that he was not in his proper position as a teacher of dancing only, and this feeling was intensified by Mr. Richardson's introduction of Mr. and Mrs. Goodwin from the Opera House, the former of whom he took as a partner with the assistance of his wife, who taught deportment, &c.

About this time an Amateur Musical Society was established, which was led and conducted by Mr. Venua, their meetings for practice were held in a large room at the George Hotel. Its members consisted of all the professional musicians, supported by the amateurs, both vocal and instrumental. At this time Mr. Venua lived at Twyford, it being a sort of central position for him, as he had teaching enough for himself and an assistant (by the name of Tyrrell) at Windsor, Eton and its neighbourhood, with appointments at Reading when he attended the amateur rehearsals. The conflicting interests of the resident musicians, and the jealousy as to who was to play first violin, tenor, and bass, made it difficult for the leader; nevertheless some good concerts were given notwithstanding these difficulties, but before the death of George the Third the Society ceased to exist.

In the year 1819 Mr. Binfield, who was at the height of his popularity, gave a musical festival which continued for three days. The sacred part of it was performed in St. Lawrence's Church and the secular in the Town Hall. The patronage Mr. Binfield received surpassed anything of the kind known to us.

The lovers of good music will not fail to be interested in hearing of the treat we had when I state that the three days' performance of sacred music consisted of Haydn's 'Creation,' the 2nd day of the 'Messiah,' and the 3rd of Handel's 'Redemption.' The best talent in the Kingdom took part at this Sacred Festival, but never shall I forget the wonderful effect produced in the sacred edifice by the singing of Miss Stephens (Countess of Essex) of 'Let the bright seraphim,' accompanied by Mr. Harper on the trumpet.

All the amateurs gave their gratuitous services, and attended several rehearsals in the large room at Mr. Binfield's house. At these I played the flute part, but at the Festival I was put in the shade by the celebrated flautist, Mr. Ireland, with Mr. Kates as second, and I was content to play an oboe part. Soon after this musical festival Mr. Venua came to live in Reading, when another Amateur Society was established, which met with very cordial public support, that gentleman not only conducting and leading the concerts, but occasionally himself playing a solo on the violin. He also frequently wrote orchestral parts for the Band, which with the Chorus consisted of about 150 persons.

The late Mr. Brain, who was an excellent singer, became our treasurer, the late Mr. Knighton, of Caversham, our secretary, and Mr. Badcock, recently deceased, the librarian. Mr. Venua also wrote two or three introductions to flute solos with orchestral accompaniments for me, and also accompaniments for the full band to a duett concertante on 'The Romance in Joseph,' the score of which I retain. This I had the pleasure of playing with the late talented Mr. Bilson Binfield in the Town Hall in the year 1830. It was composed and arranged by Berbeignier for flute and piano. This Amateur Society became very popular, and was at the height of its prosperity about the period of the erection of the Berkshire Hospital.

Much good was done sometimes by the Society giving a concert for the benefit of some unfortunate but respectable person. An instance of this occurred to the family of the late Mr. Andrews, an engineer who played 2nd flute and was a good musician. He was taken ill and died, leaving a widow with two daughters. A concert was given for their benefit, which proved a great success. I was entrusted with the funds, which were placed in the Savings Bank, and I am sure it will be known with pleasure that owing to good management on the part of the widow she was enabled to educate and place in the world her two daughters.

Our leader, Mr. Venua, having taken a residence in Albion Place, greater facilities were afforded him to attend rehearsals, and some few of us formed a Septept Party, which frequently met at his house for the enjoyment of the good compositions of Mozart, Haydn and Beethoven. I know of none of these seven persons being in existence at this time, with the exception of Mr. Butler, sen., artist, who played violoncello or double bass as the necessity arose.

We had several gentlemen amateurs - Major Fuller, Capt. Macdonald, two solicitors (Messrs. Vines), all of whom, with our talented leader, have passed away, and so has the Amateur Society.

After an interval a new Musical Society sprang into existence under the fostering influence of the Rev. Purey-Cust, now Dean of York, whose organist became our indefatigable and talented leader of the Philharmonic Society. Its success has been greatly promoted by the kind interest taken in it by the present Vicar of St. Mary's, Rev. Canon Garry. Although some ten years have elapsed since your correspondent withdrew from taking part in these Concerts, he heartily enjoyed the last one.

In describing my recollections of our musical societies during the last 75 years, I ought not to omit to state that the amateur societies to which I belonged not only gave occasional concerts for some charitable purpose, but also rendered their services at the performances of Dr. Valpy's boys at Reading School, at the triennial visitations from St. John's College, Oxford. At the time that these entertainments occurred there was direct communication from his School to the lower floor of the old Town Hall, where the Theatre was arranged. At the time there were windows looking north on the same floor, which are now closed, by whom I know not. The last time I remember to have taken part in these musical arrangements was probably 63 years ago. Dr. Valpy's eldest daughter, Mrs. Culpepper, controlled everything. The pieces chosen were a translation of a Greek play and the 'Rehearsal.' In the former, a talented pupil of the name of Richardson created quite a sensation by his performance, particularly in the scene where he falls on his knees before the King (who had ordered the destruction of his sight) and implores his mercy: 'Oh, spare my eyes if it is only to look on thee.' The late Rev. Mr. Cameron, as also Mr. Bulley, the late President of Magdalen College, Oxford, and others I could name, but probably not now living, took part in this entertainment. The orchestra consisted of all the local professors of music of any standing, as also of some amateurs, none of whom, I regret to state, are now living, excepting myself. The following gentlemen I remember to have assisted in the musical department:- Monsieur Venua, leader and conductor; Mr. Binfield, sen., and Mr. Packer, 1st violins; Mr. Bilson Binfield and Mr. Richardson, 2nd violins; Major Fuller and Mr. Goodwin, tenors; Mr. W.S. Darter, flute; Binfield, a nephew, and Mr. Tanner, violoncellos; Mr. Abery, double bass; Mr. Barkshire and Mr. Burton, French horns.

During the incumbency of the late Dr. Wise, it was customary on New Year's Eve for the ringers of St. Lawrence's parish to ring a few peals of changes and leave the bells up on their stays, and a short time before midnight to return. At the same time the Militia Band assembled at the upper part of London Street, and all was still, until the moment of St. Lawrence's clock began to strike twelve, when off went the merry peal of eight bells, and at the same moment three loud strokes of the big drum led off the Berkshire Band down London Street to the Market Place, and from thence through a portion of the town. Seventy-one years have elapsed since I first experienced the magic effect of this music of the band and the merry peal of St. Lawrence's bells breaking out in the stillness of midnight, suggesting that the old year had passed away, and welcoming the dawn of its successor. After a short interval, the old watchman, Norcroft, went up London Street, calling out 'Past twelve and a starlight mornin'.'

— 8 —

Crime and Punishment

Greyfriars Prison - whipping at the cart's tail - agricultural riots in Berkshire - trial of William Winterbourne.

Our criminal laws at that time were a disgrace to the country. Offenders were whipped, put in the stocks or pillory, for trifling offences. Some were hung for crimes which now would receive a sentence of six or twelve months imprisonment. I will mention an instance or two which came within my own knowledge, and which caused us all deep sorrow. A man of very respectable appearance was tried at our March Assizes in 1815 and found guilty of 'putting off' forged £1 notes (at Wallingford, I believe), and was left for execution. I happened to be near the gaol about this time and saw two young females, draped in mourning, leave the prison; they had been to see their father for the last time, and were so dreadfully distressed that I could not refrain from tears. On the 25th of the same month I witnessed his execution. Anything more solemn or distressing I cannot conceive. The scaffold was erected just opposite the principal entrance to the Abbey, and which at that time was also the approach to the National Schools. There was a meadow of considerable size between it and the old gaol; this space was crowded with sympathising spectators, and when the procession came on the platform, I noticed that the Governor (Mr. Eastaff) was so deeply affected that he was obliged to hold by the rails. When the prisoner (John Newbank) appeared, people seemed to hold their breath, and there was a solemn and distressing silence, but Mr. Newbank was less affected than any of those who attended him; he appeared to me to be about 50 years of age, and a little bald; when he was placed under the drop he looked at the vast and sympathising crowd, and said in a firm voice 'God bless you all.' This induced a spontaneous sort of groan from the multitude, and when the Lord's Prayer was said, as I think I never heard it before, by Dr. Barry (although Dr. Williams might have been the gaol chaplain), most if not

84

Reading Market Place about 1840.

all of the people kneeled and at the close of the prayer responded with a solemn 'Amen.'

I wish to introduce at this time what I ought to have done when writing about the Abbey. I allude to the beautiful ruin of Grey Friars as it was 70 years since. Even then it was a most interesting object notwithstanding the spoilers' efforts to destroy it. A future generation will wonder what state of civilization existed in England during the reign of George the Third, that it should have been permitted for such a beautiful church, as this must have been, standing as it did in a situation where an additional one was required, to be allowed to fall to pieces. What is worse was the base use to which it was eventually appropriated. Our forefathers when 'jumping about the woods with painted faces' would hardly have been such barbarians. In the first place I may state that as far back as my memory serves me, and long before the railways were thought of there was a good deal of land which surrounded Grey

Friars, embracing what is now named Grey Friars Road; and on the Caversham Road side it reached beyond the railway bridge; there were also large trees standing on the meadow which many now living must remember. The first interference with this ruin (in my life time) was the destruction of the chancel for the purpose of making room for a servants' office or kitchen to a new house which was erected by Mr. Lancelot Austwick, then a member of the Corporation. I do not remember anything of importance in reference to the place as a prison prior to the punishment by the whipping of Browne, the hairdresser, but I wish to state the condition of the prison in its interior when I first saw it. I was accompanied by Mr. John Cocks, the late senior partner in the Reading Sauce Establishment, who wished to have an interview with a person confined there for debt, and whose father was, some years earlier, one of the most respected tradesmen in Reading; he and his family having resided in the Market Place for a long period. The gaoler's house consisted of a sitting room, kitchen and two bedrooms, and no outlet or garden. The whole area of the Church was sub-divided into different cells; the best of them were appropriated to the debtors, but even these were unfit for human beings to sleep in. I noticed that the partitions were partly of wood, and almost all the available white-washed surface of the partitions was written on by the prisoners in pencil. Most of it was abusive of those who were instrumental in depriving them of their liberty. The whole structure was very frail and many of the criminal class managed to escape. The once beautiful columns were utilized as supports to the roof of this hideous structure, and much of its beauty was hidden by patches of brickwork. The lovely west window was defaced by having some of the openings filled in with red brickwork; others were open.

In the year 1851, I, at a public meeting, drew attention to the wretched condition of this prison. Twenty-six years had elapsed since I saw the place as just described, and now I, at the request of the late Mr. Geo. May, accompanied him there to see a young man who was supposed to be insane, he having threatened to take his father's life; the result was the immediate removal of him to Littlemore. At this time (1851) I saw no alteration in the appearance of the prison beyond that which the lapse of time would occasion. All these abominations are now removed, and a new Church (in which the ruins of the Old Grey Friars are incorporated) has been erected, to the great gratification of us all.

The keeper of Grey Friars Prison, about the year 1816, was a person of the name of Paradise. I don't know that he was of a cruel disposition, but he was compelled to do the bidding of his superiors, and sometimes his occupation was far from being in harmony with his name. I have in previous papers alluded to some of the outrageous sentences passed on criminals for trifling offences, and I will now relate one which occurred, and Paradise had to inflict the punishment. It was the most cruel that I have ever seen recorded in this or any other country. A man of the labouring class, living on the west side of Silver Street, in one of those old houses which have overhanging eaves, and where the ground floors are much below the level of the road, situate next to the stable yard of the Greyhound public house, had been out of work for some time and in want of food. In passing up Castle Street he stole a loaf of bread from the shop of a baker of the name of Turner. He was apprehended, tried and sentenced by Martin Annesley to be publicly whipped at the cart's tail from the Grey Friars Prison to his cottage in Silver Street. He was stripped to his waist, and he had to walk behind a horse and cart with his hands so tied that he could not alter his position. I was standing near the post office in London Street, when my attention was drawn to an approaching crowd, and until that moment I was not in the least aware of what occasioned the excitement. When the crowd arrived opposite our house, I ran to see the cause of it. I then witnessed a shocking sight; what no one at this period would have supposed possible to have been permitted in England. There was not a portion of this poor fellow's back that was not literally cut to shreds; his sufferings were dreadful, and with the blood running down, it presented a dreadful and sickening sight. I merely followed at a distance to see where they took him. I have witnessed distressing sights since this occurrence, particularly at the time of the accident, more than 40 years since, in the Great Western Sonning Hill cutting, when about a dozen persons were killed and many injured. As I was living at the time near the scene, I rode quickly there and assisted as well as I could in laying the dead on the slopes; but even this sight, terrible as it was, did not affect me like the one I have narrated. In point of fact, the poor fellow, for merely stealing a loaf, was whipped to death, for he never left his room alive; therefore, for this trifling offence, this man was punished to a greater extent than would have happened had he committed murder. As soon as it became known that death had resulted, the subject was spoken of in severe terms by every one, and it was also remarked that there ought to have been a medical man present to have stopped the infliction of the cat so soon as it became dangerous. But, as far as I saw, there was no cessation of punishment whatever, notwithstanding the victim's cries. At this period there was a Mr. Dawers, residing in St. Giles's parish, a literary man, but of whom I knew little. It seems that he saw something of the case, and was induced to write an article, which appeared in a newspaper, wherein he denounced the conduct of Mr. Annesley, and indeed all the magistrates, for allowing such a crime to be committed in the name of justice. This led to the author's name being made known, and a criminal information was the consequence. Mr. Dawers having consulted his friends, and it not being of importance where he lived, left the town rather than incur the expense of defending himself or running the risk of imprisonment. I think that this gentleman was not heard of in Reading again, but went to live on the other side of the Channel. A year or two after the departure of Mr. Dawers, it was stated that he was a Government pensioner, he having given information which led to the apprehension of Col. Despard, who was executed for high treason.

About 1830, the agricultural labourers took it into their heads that the introduction of machinery for thrashing, hay-making &c., was the cause of keeping down their wages, and of lessening the amount of labour. This feeling was aggravated by the free use of beer which they obtained by going from farm to farm and using threats. Some other men for the sake of drink joined the labourers, and at last they began breaking up these machines. Great alarm was felt in Reading, it being feared that the rioting would reach the town owing to the number of the disaffected. The authorities here became alarmed, and it was thought necessary to apply for a company of Foot Guards from Windsor. In consequence of this application a body of the Guards came to Reading, and on a Sunday some of them sat in St. Giles' Church chancel with their fire-locks. From what I afterwards heard from a person residing in the disturbed neighbourhood, a couple of dozen constables could have suppressed the movement at once as far as this part of the country was concerned. The military were not required to act, but many of the rioters were taken into custody by the civil power without personal injury being sustained by anyone. Those men who were known to be the most active were committed for trial, and eventually the Government sent a Special Commission (consisting of three Judges) to try these men at Reading before proceeding to Abingdon. The Commission consisted of Mr. Justice Park, Baron Bolland, and Mr. Justice Patteson, who took lodgings at the Crown Hotel.

Most of the prisoners who were found guilty were transported for life, and three were sentenced to be executed, viz., William Oakley, William Winterbourne, and Alfred Darling. On the evening of the departure of the Judges there was a public dinner, at which I was present with probably fifty others, and the late Mr. Robert Palmer, of Reading, was Chairman. As we were taking dessert, an elderly gentleman and his son, both of whom belonged to the Society of Friends, came into the room, and the elder of the two, in an apologetic manner, addressed the Chairman, and expressed a hope that neither he nor the company would feel offended at their intruding at such a moment, but they had an urgent appeal to make, and no time must be lost. They stated that the Judges who had tried the prisoners referred to had ordered that the execution should take place a few days hence, I think about five, not allowing them to live so long as they would have done had they committed murder. This statement aroused the indignation of all present, and at once it was determined to raise a subscription in the room, and, if possible, save the lives of these men. After a brief consultation I undertook to ride down to Coley Park and seek the assistance and advice of Mr. Monck. I was fortunate enough to find him at home, and he received me very courteously. I explained to him what had occurred, and he very kindly wrote a letter of introduction for me to the Earl of Abingdon and also wrote one to Lord Amesbury. On my return to the Inn, I found a post-chaise and four horses at the door. I entered the room and explained the advice given me by Mr. Monck, also that the Judges had gone to Abingdon and would open the Commission there the next morning. It was felt that not a moment should be lost, but the question was, who should go. I was pressed to take the letters of introduction, depart at once, and do my best. In the end, I and the young friend left together, he having consented to accompany me. We immediately started in the post-chaise referred to, and as the post-boys had heard what our object was their sympathies were in harmony with ours, and we arrived at Abingdon in an incredibly short time. We were too late to obtain an interview with the Judges, but were successful in presenting our letters our letters of introduction to the Earl of Abingdon and Lord Amesbury, from whom we received letters to the Judges. We retired to our hotel, but the excitement of our enterprise had deprived us of the power to sleep. Having ascertained the hour that their Lordships would be at breakfast, we waited on them and presented our letters of introduction, which Justice Park looked at, and passed them to his colleagues. Baron Bolland said, 'Before we left Reading we gave the most anxious consideration to these cases, and we have selected three of the worst of the offenders for capital punishment.' Baron Park interposed, and, with emphasis, said, 'If his Majesty allows these fellows to escape I would recommend him to open all the gaols in the Kingdom.' We pleaded hard for some secondary punishment, anything rather than that their lives should be sacrificed. We ventured to state that we were entreated by our fellow-townsmen to seek an interview with their Lordships to sue for mercy on behalf of these misguided men, and that as soon as it was announced that an order had been issued for their execution, great excitement was apparent in the town. Baron Park replied, 'We have made our report, and you must now apply to Lord Melbourne; we have nothing more to do with it.' I said, 'My Lords, we have a memorial signed by the prosecutor and the Petit Jury who tried the case in question. Will you allow the Lord Lieutenant, the Earl of Abingdon, to sign it?' 'Certainly not,' said Baron Park, 'he is one of the Commission.' 'Or Lord Amesbury?' 'No, he also is one of the Commission.' It was easy enough to see that Baron Park was determined, if possible, that the executions should take place, so we left, and it being about the time for the arrival of the Grand Jury, we waited at their hotels, and in the course of the morning succeeded in obtaining the signatures of all of them but one, who came from Wallingford, and he said he would place his arm on a block and have it chopped off before he would sign it. I merely doffed my hat and said nothing, but if he were living I would mention his name.

Having done all we could we returned to the inn, and in doing so met Mr. Rigby, the prisoners' counsel, and all three of us returned in post-chaise to Reading. On our arrival we found that petitions had been placed in different parts of the town, and when they were put together I really believe they would have reach across the Market Place. The next thing was to see Mr. Monck and induce him to proceed to London to see Lord Melbourne. This he readily acceded to, but Lord Melbourne said, on seeing the petition, 'I do not like to present this large petition; it looks like intimidation.' Mr. Monck replied, 'I have another signed by the prosecutor and the jury who tried the case, and also nearly all the grand jury.' Lord Melbourne said, 'I will take this to the King'; the result being that two were saved, but Winterbourne was executed. I omitted to mention that one argument we used with the Judges was that no personal violence was sustained by any one, but Baron Park warmly replied, 'They held bludgeons over people's heads.' I am not aware that any one of these convicts ever returned to their homes or country.

— 9 —
The Poor

Sufferings of the poor - work of the Philanthropic Institution - misfortunes of some old aquaintances.

The approaching winter of 1888 will I fear be accompanied by a considerable amount of suffering amongst the working classes, unless employment is provided for them. I hope I may infer from the constitution of the Board of Guardians, that, if necessary, they will adopt a judicious and extended system of out-door relief, as by this course they may prevent much sickness and suffering.

I venture to hope that through the exertions of lady visitors all cases of real distress will be reported by them, so that our feelings may not be outraged by hearing of a fellow creature dying from starvation here, as has recently occurred in London in close proximity to the residences of the wealthy. What ever may be the fate of the Corporation Bill, I venture to hope that an immediate understanding will be arrived at between the Thames Commissioners and the local authority; so that 'Silly Bridge' may be re-built, and the towing path put into proper repair. This course would give work to many, and relieve the rates. With reference to the bridge the re-building of which has occurred within my memory and which must have been paid for out of public funds by some constituted body, up to this time I believe no record of it has been found. Perhaps this allusion to the subject may be the means of discovering who the builders were. My impression is that the work was done by the late Mr. Ball and Mr. Biggs. Even if the expense of the re-building of the bridge and the dredging of the Kennet from the 'Six Bells' to the Lock below (which will probably be necessary) were wholly to devolve upon the rate payers, it would be much better to spend money at this season of the year in that way rather than in the demoralizing way of charity.

With reference to the Philanthropic Institution, and its usefulness at this season of the year, when so many of the industrious classes are thrown out of work, I have had long experience. This statement will not be controverted when I mention the fact that I have been a member of the original institution and a subscriber to its funds since the 27th November, 1823, or 65 years to the time of my writing this, viz., October, 1888. I would, therefore, earnestly recommend to those who have the heart and ability to contribute towards the necessities of those in poverty and suffering, to do so through the medium of this or some kindred society. If this suggestion were adopted, instead of indiscriminate charity, donors would have the happiness of knowing the good they had done. From the stringency of its rules I never knew an instance of the society being imposed upon. It does not give to those who receive parochial relief, but to deserving working men and mechanics who are sometimes overtaken by sudden illness, or struggling through a period of adversity.

In the early days I often took an active part in the proceedings before a Committee, sometimes presenting a petition for their consideration, at other times acting as a visitor. At the period referred to there were very few resident gentlemen or respectable tradesmen in the town who were not subscribers or members. The annual dinner used to be attended by the Mayor, Magistrates, and some members of the Corporation, neighbouring gentry and Borough members. About the year 1836, Sergt. Talfourd presided, the Vice-Chairman being C.S. Robinson, Esq., of Caversham; also Capt. Montagu, Dr. Mitford, the Hon. Capt. Gore and Mr. Chas. Russell, M.P. Upon the occasion referred to Mr. Russell, returning thanks in response to his health having been drunk, made a most happy and graceful allusion to the loss the town had sustained by the death of his late friend and colleague Mr. J. Berkeley Monck, a sentiment which was heartily reciprocated by all of us. The mention of the name of Mr. Chas. Russell reminds me of an incident which occurred at a public dinner of the Benevolent Institution (which was an off-shoot of the Philanthropic Institution, and of kindred character) about the year 1828. Mr. Chas. Russell, who at the time was one of our representatives, in returning thanks for the toast of his health, apologised for his brother's, Sir Henry Russell's, absence, in a singularly happy strain. He said that his brother's absence was due to the fact that Lady Russell had that day presented him with a son, a free born English

View of London Street showing the New Public Hall and Lovejoy's bookshop about 1840.

child. (I may mention that the slavery question was at the time to which I refer occupying a good deal of public attention.) This event he contrasted with the slave mother, who had gone through the same perils only to present her husband with a slave child, who, at any time, might be torn from her embrace and sold like one of the cattle in the field.

The good work of the Philanthropic Institution is still going on, and deserves to be well supported by the present generation; it is sad to think that probably there is no one who was a member of it in the year 1823, when I was a member, who is now living. A least I do not know one.

It may not be out of place if I here record one instance out of many which occurred during the first thirty years of my membership. I was solicited by a gentleman to present a petition on behalf of a journeyman cabinet maker, who lived in Laud Place, and was stricken down with illness. I acceded to his request, as he was a subscriber. Mr. Chas. Strudwick, the Secretary, read the petition at a full meeting. The Chairman requested any two gentlemen who knew anything of the case to volunteer their services as visitors, and to report upon it to the Committee. This was done, and in the result I was entrusted with three pounds, with a request that I should use my own discretion as to its application. From what I knew of the case I first ordered some coal, and shortly afterwards visited the family. I found a woman at the door, to whom I mentioned the object of my visit; she, good creature, had gone to the afflicted family as a neighbour, and had done what she could for them, she herself being too poor to do more than give her gratuitous services. I found the head of the family looking very ill, and far from convalescent; at that moment no fire; the young wife in bed with an infant a fortnight old ; two children on the floor of about the age of four and six years. Although there was neither fire nor food, there was an appearance of order and cleanliness. I found that all the husband's savings had gone to pay rent, that his tools and a blanket had been pawned, and there was no food in the house. I, too quickly I fear, made known to them the good news that their petition had been favourably received, and that I was entrusted with the funds for their relief. On enquiring of the young mother if they had any food in the house she burst into tears, for they had none. The children, seeing their mother weep, began to cry and hold on by the bedclothes. The husband was so moved by this, that in attempting to express his gratitude he broke down and sobbed convulsively. I think that I never felt so unmanned, for the whole scene was a painful one. I turned my attention to the little ones, as I had some sweets in my pocket. The good-hearted neighbour had gone, by my directions, to buy grocery, &c., and on her return lighted a fire and made some tea. I consulted with them as to the redemption of the bedding, &c., also about the tools, but these were not immediately required. My impression was that if this timely relief had not been afforded them the husband would not have recovered, for they would rather have starved than applied to the parish for relief.

I dwell on this scene as it presented itself to me, as I saw it on the night in question, but before I left all was changed, and joy was depicted on the countenances of even the little ones. With the promise that I would express their gratitude to the Society, I left them. My visits were continued until the husband recovered and resumed work, and with a little additional help from time to time the family became well and happy.

In recording past events that have occurred in my native town of Reading, changes of the most interesting, and sometimes of a painful character, have happened to members of families resident here. Some of those I refer to were, like myself, far from wealthy when I first knew them; but by perseverance and honourable industry have acquired fortunes, and it is due to them to state that there is no institution or good work to be performed which has the tendency to promote the moral and material welfare of the people to which they are not most liberal contributors.

But, alas! there is another side of the picture, for I also remember families who once held a good social position, and were looked up to as leading people of influence, who in the course of time were reduced to a very humble position; some of them as a last resort seeking refuge in our Union Workhouse. I cannot for obvious reasons allude to these; but I venture to mention three cases of persons who I should designate of the middle class. A disastrous fire occurred on the premises of Mr. Nicholson, a wholesale cork merchant of Friar Street, in May, 1812, at which I saw the carcase of a valuable horse amongst the ruins. The destruction of the premises was complete, and I believe nothing could be saved. The landlord of the Boar's Head Inn opposite told the person who had the care of me that the cries of the imprisoned horse were extremely distressing, and could be heard a great way off. A short time afterwards I saw two gentlemen with Mr. Nicholson on High Bridge. I was going to school, and stopped to look over the coping at a person trolling for barbel, when I overheard these gentlemen soliciting another for a subscription for Mr. Nicholson, he having neglected to insure his premises, and lost everything. I know not what the result was, but Mr. Nicholson eventually left Reading, and his son, with a partner, occupied premises and carried on cork-cutting on the site where now stands Cock's Sauce Establishment in Duke Street. These premises were pulled down about the year 1821, and the present structure was erected on oak piles by Mr. Bailey, an architect of London, who at the same period was engaged with extensive alterations to Caversham Park Mansion. This Mr. Nicholson, jun., was a member of the Woodley Troop, and was considered to be the best swordsman in it. About thirty-six years after the fire referred to, I was engaged in conversation with the late Mr. William Brown, architect, at the Workhouse in Friar's Place, when I saw poor old Mr. Nicholson brought here in a horse and cart to end his days in the Union; it was, for me, who remembered his former position, a painful spectacle.

Another case occurred to a person who was managing clerk (in my time) to two firms of solicitors who were at the head of the profession in Reading. He had saved a considerable sum and had bought a house in London Street, which was rated at £60 per annum. This residence was put in thorough repair, and the gentleman referred to married and occupied it for some years. During his occupation, or soon afterwards, his wife died, and the husband had a vault and handsome tomb erected in St. Giles' Churchyard facing Horn Street, into which her remains were placed. At this period the Blagrave title was esteemed (by our sagacious lawyers) to be better than freehold. When a lease was originally granted three lives were introduced, and when one life fell in a sum of money had to be paid for the insertion of another. In the case I am discussing two lives had passed away without being renewed, and now the last was gone. An application was in due course made to Col. Blagrave to allow a renewal of the three lives alluded to, but the Colonel refused. At all events the lessee having exhausted conciliatory means was driven to apply to the Court of Chancery at his own cost (an imprudent step as we now know), for his was the worst case to litigate upon, he having neglected to renew when the first life fell in. There were others who, with only one life gone, could, with the pecuniary help of other lessees, have fought the battle more successfully. As it was, he sustained a crushing defeat, had to pay the costs and lost all his property. This decision of the Lord Chancellor's was a great misfortune for those who held these leases, as also to the trade of Reading, from which it was years in recovering. Messrs. Cocks' extensive premises in Duke Street, and those of the late Alderman Lewis, at the corner of the Market Place, were erected nearly at the same period, and were very expensive structures; both have now fallen into the hands of the Blagrave family, to whom I hear a heavy rent is paid.

The unfortunate litigant, to whom I have alluded, never again looked up, but ended his days in the Workhouse. Had it not been for the kindness of friends who paid the expenses of his funeral, he would have had a pauper's grave; but his most fervent wishes have been given effect to, and he is now at rest in the vault with the wife of his first love.

The most singular event of my life which I have in my memory refers to the year 1817. I mentioned earlier having seen the Queen of George the Third, accompanied by Princess Augusta, pass through Reading on their way to Bath, changing horses at the Crown Hotel. Soon afterwards the lamented death of the Princess Charlotte occurred at the age of 22, leaving a husband (Prince Leopold) and the whole nation in deep sorrow. No public event in my time ever produced such a universal union of spontaneous sympathy. All business was suspended and shops closed; blinds were drawn down to the windows of private houses, and even the poorest of the poor wore some humble token of sympathy. The nation's brightest hope was that the Princess would become our Queen and leave a successor in the person of her offspring; but it happened otherwise, for both mother and babe died, and so grieved was her medical attendant that it was stated that he committed suicide. As may be supposed, special services were held at churches and chapels on the day of the Princess's funeral. On this occasion a service was held at the newly-erected Unitarian Chapel in London Street (now known as St. Giles' Hall). It was made known that a celebrated minister named Trevelyan would preach the funeral sermon. The choir had a square space allotted to them in the centre of the chapel, and were members of the congregation; the instrumentalists were mostly professionals. It was arranged that appropriate anthems should be sung, in which occurred duets for treble voices. They had a very good first treble in the person of a lady, and as I was pretty well known to have a tolerably good treble voice, I, with the permission of my father, did my best as second. On the day in question the chapel was filled to suffocation. This led to the service being repeated, and one of the anthems was 'Vital Spark of Heavenly Flame.' It was also known as 'Pope's Ode.' Upon this occasion the place was again overcrowded.

I am not aware of ever having spoken to or seen the person with whom I sang from that time until about four years since, when I, for the first time, looked through the wards of our Union. The Mistress of the establishment was good enough to accompany me through the building, and most of the inmates of both sexes seemed to recognise me. On arriving at the Infirmary (which contained about 14 beds), I was struck with admiration at the cleanliness and order of it - the space between the beds and the excellent ventilation of the place. All the inmates were aged people to whom I spoke, for some of them knew me, and on arriving at the last bed I found a female sitting in a chair by its side, who politely rose as I approached, and on being asked by the Mistress if I was known to her, she said 'Yes, it is Mr. —.' I said 'Pray, how is it that you know me?' At this remark she became somewhat animated, and I seemed to recognise her features, for I said 'Your name is —,' to which she replied in the affirmative. This unfortunate person was the one who sang with me in 1817. She had lost all her property, I believe, by an unfortunate investment, and, broken-hearted, she came to the place of her birth, and, having no relative living or friend she remembered, sought refuge in Reading Union, where I saw her after an interval of nearly 70 years. As may be supposed, I did what little I could to make her life tolerable, but the Governor's wife was very kind to her till her death, which occurred in her 83rd year.

—10—
Public Works

Reading waterworks - public health enquiry - introduction of gas lighting.

The subject of water supply is an important one, and was so considered at an early period of this century, and there were some spasmodic and abortive attempts made by the then Water Company to supply this essential element to health. I remember as far back as 1814 that a large lead reservoir stood in the centre of Broad Street opposite the Wool Pack Inn, which was supplied with water by means of a three-action pump fixed in Mill Lane; its distribution being through wooden pipes. The only other means of obtaining water was from wells and pumps, but as some wells were 30 to 90 feet in depth, it was not only expensive but a very laborious affair to raise it by means of force-pumps to the upper stories of a house.

The wooden pipes to which I refer were simply elm trees, selected for straightness, and these were prepared by two men named Sley and Morris; the former resided at the north end of East Street, and the pipes were bored and otherwise completed on these premises; the section of the old house is still visible on the gable of the adjoining one, but the site is now occupied by some new cottages.

The mode adopted was to lay the trees horizontally on stiff tressels, and then apply a three or four-inch augur with long rod and a handle from six to seven feet long. This gave the men sufficient power to bore the pipes, the small end of which was tapered so as to enter the large end of another, and when laid the swelling of the timber made the joints water-tight. Three-quarter inch lead pipes (with a ferrule inserted in the wooden ones) branched off to the different houses within the power of this primitive mode of supply. If a fire occurred a plug had to be pulled up from the main, and dams were formed so as to supply an engine with the aid of leathern buckets, and if a burst occurred this process of pulling up a plug had to be adopted, consequently no supply could be obtained for a whole district until the said repairs were effected. Constant obstructions occurred from fish. &c., getting into the branch pipes, and upon one occasion whilst talking to the late Dr. Hooper in London Street, who himself was not only a shareholder, but took an active part in the management, Mr. John Middleton, an inn-keeper, came up and complained to the Dr. of the insufficient supply of water to his house and that he was frequently obliged to employ a plumber to force back eels and fish which stopped the lead pipes into his house. The only satisfaction he obtained from the Dr. was, that he had to be congratulated in having a supply of fish without being called upon to pay for it. Some years subsequent to this a reservoir was erected near the entrance to Coley Avenue, but in a short time this came to grief, causing considerable damage.

In 1820, Mr. Cubitt, an eminent engineer, erected the present water tower, which enabled the Company to supply some of the houses in a higher position, and he also increased the pumping power in Mill Lane, but did not provide filter beds. The supply was on alternate days, and was pumped from a very questionable source. In 1846, there was much sickness in the town, which induced some of the inhabitants to inquire as to the cause. It happened in the autumn of this year that, after a storm, I saw the water in Mill Lane from whence the town was supplied in such a filthy state that I wrote a letter to the *Reading Mercury* on the subject.

It will probably be remembered by some that in 1847 an inquiry as to the sanitary state of Reading, and also as to the desirability of carrying out a system of drainage and better supply of water, was held in the New Hall in London Street, before J.K. Rickards and John Shaw, Esqrs., Mr. Keating being engaged on behalf of the town, and Mr. Warren for the promoters of the scheme. The latter, in a sensational speech, said that 'he stood between the Dead and the Living.' I had to appear and give evidence, which resulted in my being obliged to answer over 200 questions. In cross-examination I was asked either by Mr. Weedon or Mr. Warren if I wrote the following letter to a local paper:

'Sir, — Allow me through the medium of your paper to call the attention of my fellow-townsmen to a few remarks I am desirous of

Thomas Noon Talfourd, M.P. for Reading 1835-41.

making in reference to the important subject of our water supply. Much has been written and said lately as to the sanitary condition of the town, and it has been stated that the exhalations from our churchyards engender fever; all this may be very true and ought to be remedied; but I will take the liberty of mentioning another grievance, not, I believe, yet alluded to, and which may fairly be considered as a powerful auxiliary in the promotion of the late epidemic. The source from which the town is supplied with water is of the most filthy description; I have this summer, during the most unhealthy period, seen the whole of the stream, from the Bridge in Horn Street to the Mill below, where the water works are situate, of a dark chocolate colour, and altogether unfit for any purpose; this river is also contaminated by being the receptacle of the drainage of Southampton and Horn Streets, also that of a tan-yard, brick-kiln, timber yard, iron foundry, &c., &c. It may be urged that the public have the remedy by sinking wells and erecting pumps; not so, however, for in many situations they have really no remedy; the supply must be from the waterworks or none, on account of the existence of innumerable cesspools which impregnate the soil to a very considerable distance. The question naturally arises, What is the remedy? I could much easier point out what to avoid than to adopt; for instance, I would say, do not have your water supply from the branch of the Kennet before referred to, as that is impure; neither from below; for in addition to the before mentioned impurities, there are those arising from the Gas Wharf; it frequently happens that fish in this part of the river are poisoned by it. Another of your correspondents has suggested that the hills near Reading would afford an abundant supply; this I think very doubtful. I have known, in dry seasons, the whole of the springs to fail there. It has occurred to me that the extensive lake at Whiteknights affords an illustration of this mode of supply; in the winter and during wet seasons there is an abundance of water, partly from landsprings, but in a great measure from superficial drainage; the superfluous water runs down the low land behind the Cemetery to the London Road, but in the summer and dry seasons, when a greater supply is required, scarcely any water for many weeks escapes the lake; this I think tolerably conclusive evidence either that the supply from this source would be insufficient or that a very extensive reservoir indeed must be formed; another objection to this mode is that in the event of the hills affording sufficient for the low parts of Reading, the reservoirs must be erected perhaps 25 feet high, or the houses on the elevated spots cannot be supplied. The

Thames, therefore, above the junction with the Kennet, seems the best adapted situation for the purpose, unless a place on the Kennet above the town can be procured. The supply from the Water Company being on alternate days, it frequently happens that the cisterns become empty; the ball-cocks in consequence do not act; the water comes on and continues running until the cesspools are filled; thus is occasioned the necessity for more frequently emptying these places, and in this way the air becomes contaminated; the soil is removed to the suburbs to undergo a process of decomposition, and eventually advertised as a manure with some new name. In conclusion, I take the liberty of stating that the necessity for pure water is as urgent as that of its being abundant; that the supply should be constant, and at such terms as to be within the reach of all; that where small tenements are erected the landlords, not the tenants, should be compelled to pay for it; thus would cleanliness and health be promoted.'

'By Mr. Warren: Did you write that letter? Yes, I did, and I believe every word of it to be true.'

It is due to the late proprietors of the Waterworks to state that subsequently to the appearance of this letter, they obtained fresh Parliamentary powers, and very materially improved the water supply by the introduction of an intermittent supply, and by the adoption of filtering beds. All this they did before the Corporation purchased their interest. The works have since been improved, which, with the perfect system of drainage (which has been introduced), has made Reading one of the healthiest towns in the United Kingdom.

The first attempt that I remember to procure Gas in Reading occurred in 1819, when a small building was erected in Gas Lane, Bridge Street, with miniature apparatus for lighting the Billiard Subscription Rooms. A few years afterwards a Company was formed, and the works were erected on the wharf adjacent. At this time the old oil lamps were removed, and the town was, for the first time, lighted with gas. It was not long before an attempt was made to induce the Company to lower the price, but without success. This led to the formation of a new Company, and, as a consequence, our roads were once more torn up and a fresh set of main pipes laid down. The competition which resulted was the cause of a good deal of irritation at the time, and some wag compared the two companies to the Old and New Magpie Inns on Hounslow Heath, where on the sign of the old house was written:

'This is the Old Magpie and the right,
The other was set up for nought but spite.'

These rival companies competed for the public lamps, as also for private supply, but in course of time the two united and the competition ceased. I think that very soon after this coalition they obtained the power of making those who lived outside the borough pay considerably more than those living in it. In the early days of the concern there might have been some justification for the extra charge, when houses were few and far between, but that arrangement cannot now apply. We must have been all asleep when their last Bill was before Parliament that we did not threaten to oppose it, unless the Company consented to reduce their charge to the price paid for it in the town.

I cannot refrain from recording a good joke that we had at the expense of the then genial Chairman of the Gas Company at the time to which I refer. It occurred at a public dinner some years since at the Great Western Hotel. After the usual loyal toasts, the Chairman rose in response to his health, and, in eloquent terms, discoursed on the advantages Reading possessed in having a Gas Company who studied to give the public a participation in their profits by keeping down the price &c.; 'and now,' said the Chairman (but this was after dinner), 'that we have obtained additional powers, you have ocular proof in this room of the superior illuminating power of gas.' This speech of my friend, who, by the bye, has a good deal of practice in this way, even now, was received with much applause. I was sitting near him, and suggested that he should not advertise his gas there; but he kept on extolling the gas - when it became apparent that something was wrong -the light began to fail, and while my friend was looking up a few more superlatives we were left in total darkness.

—11—
Politics

*Parliamentary elections - the age of reform - reminiscences of
some Members for the borough - a Free Trade meeting at the
Town Hall.*

Perhaps there is no town in the United Kingdom where there have
been more severe political contests fought than in Reading. The
knowledge I have of the elections preceding my time came to me on
tradition from a maiden aunt who died in the year 1838 at the age of 78,
and who resided her whole life at Wargrave. What interested me most
as a boy was her description of Lord Barrymore and his theatre, at which
she was a frequent visitor, and of the great people who came to it from
London either as amateur performers or as guests.

At one time his Lordship was determined to represent Reading if he
could, for the lady in question informed me that he and a party of
friends started from Wargrave in a carriage with four horses, on a
Sunday afternoon, for the purpose of contesting the election which (so I
understood her) was to occur on the following day, and he was defeated
by only a slender majority. The other candidates were Mr. Annesley and
the Hon. Mr. Neville (a son of Lord Braybrooke). It is perhaps not
generally known that after Lord Barrymore's fatal accident, Wargrave
Theatre was pulled down and a great part of the building material used
in the erection of Marsh Place, West Street. In confirmation of this, I
myself saw, in the year 1818, some ornamental fittings which were not
consistent with the style of the houses, all of which at that time were
private residences, and belonged to the family of Dr. Marsh.

The first election of which I had any idea must have been about the
year 1807, when I resided near the Crown Hotel, which was the head-
quarters of Charles Shaw-Lefevre, the father of the present Lord
Eversley, whose features I remember so well that I could recognise his

portrait in a moment. This reminds me that the senior Mr. Vines, solicitor, Broad Street, had in 1818 an excellent portrait in oil of this Mr. Lefevre. Mr. Vines was his agent. At this election of 1807 I only remember being dressed with the Lefevre colours, and seeing a lot of garland women emerge from Silver Street led by a woman, who I in after years knew as a Mrs. Welman, wife of a noted horse breaker.

The next election I witnessed was that of 1812. Mr. Monck at this time was residing in France, and the Liberals determined that there should be no walk over. They, however, at the time were not prepared with a candidate. A meeting was held, at which it was decided to send Mr. Warry, of Minster Street, to France, to endeavour to prevail on Mr. Monck to contest the borough. Mr. Monck did return, and at the election which followed, the result was:- Lefevre, 439; Simeon 391; Monck, 286.

It will be observed that Mr. Simeon defeated Mr. Monck by a majority of 105. The Simeon family at this time were very popular in Reading, and in recording the events of 1812 it occurred to me that one at least of the family was buried in St. Giles' original churchyard, in an expensively constructed vault with iron railings. It is situated in the N.E. corner, and to my personal knowledge it has been two or three times repaired and otherwise restored within the last 70 years. In writing these recollections of by-gone days, I thought I would stay my hand and visit the said tomb. This I did on Wednesday, the 19th of May instant, and I regret to state that the whole structure is disgracefully neglected; in fact, it is fast going to decay. My impression is that a sum of money was invested for the express purpose of keeping this vault in repair.

To revert again to the election of 1812, the Tory party brought all their strength to bear upon Mr. Monck. It was stated incorrectly that he was a Roman Catholic, that the Pope was his friend, from whom he had received a concordat, and he was by his opponents honoured with the title of the 'Monck of Tours.' There was a good deal of treating, and, I fear, bribery at this election, so the Liberals issued handbills as follows: 'Caution, those suspected of being base enough to receive bribes will be watched.' 'The bribery oath will be administered, take care.' 'Those who advocate purity of election, poll early for Lefevre and Monck.'

At this time the Blue party, just before the election, distributed beer pretty freely. In London Street a butt of strong beer was drawn on a truck and left opposite the Barley Mow. A clumsy fellow in tapping it lost a lot, which escaped into the gutter, and some of the roughs drank from this source and became drunk; others took as much as they pleased from the cask. Mrs. Welman, the garland woman, amused the people by calling out 'Here is a Bill, no bribery in it. Why bless ye, they be pretty near all bribed, and I don't blame 'em I wishes I was a voter, I would get all I could out of 'em, for they makes a nice thing of it when they do get into Parliament.'

The exciting scene which followed induced people to put up their shutters, and I made my escape home for the purpose of looking on from a window. A gentleman by the name of Cutter was imprudent enough to come down London Street with a rosette of Mr. Monck's colours on his breast, and when opposite Simeon's party they rushed upon him to take away his colours, but he fought his way bravely until he reached the shop of Mr. Tagg, the upholsterer (now Gilbert), when Mr. Tagg opened the door and pulled him in. Mr. Cutter was not much hurt, but he lost his rosette (and his temper), and had his hat knocked over his eyes. The Mr. Henry Tagg here referred to died in 1813, and was succeeded by Messrs. Shotter and White. Mr. Tagg's brother was proprietor of the 'Old Bear' Posting Inn, in Bridge Street; he died in 1817, and both were buried in the N.W. corner of St. Giles' Churchyard.

At the general election of 1818 Chas. Fyshe Palmer became a candidate in conjunction with Mr. Lefevre, and they were opposed by Mr. Weyland, of Hawthorn Hill. This contest, like the one in 1812, was fought with great vigour, but it resulted in placing Lefevre at the head of the poll by a large majority. His colours were purple, Fyshe Palmer assumed the orange with a cockle shell in the centre, and Mr. Weyland the blue. The numbers at the close were: For Lefevre, 520; Palmer, 379; Weyland, 303.

After an interval of only two years, occurred the election of 1820. The candidates for Reading were Monck, Palmer and Weyland. The attack on Fyshe Palmer's seat, in consequence of Lady Madelina Palmer's pension (which might have disqualified him) having failed, the

Strong Beer,
My Boys!

TO THE

Mechanics & Labourers.

Friends and Fellow Countrymen,

YOUR Votes will determine who shall be the Members for READING.

The price of STRONG BEER more particularly concerns you than any other class of Society. Mr. PALMER and Mr. MONCK caused the price to be reduced from *Six-pence* to *Four-pence* per Quart. It is necessary you should all perfectly understand, that

The Man, who supports Messrs. Palmer and Monck, votes for Beer at Four-pence per Quart!

The Man, who supports Messrs. Wakefield and Spence, votes for Beer to be raised to Six-pence per Quart!

For, if either of these Adventurers should be returned, advantage will soon be taken of some Excise Bill, to introduce a Clause by way of rider, as it is called, putting such resrictions on the Retail Breweries, that it will be impossible to carry them on!

From your Friend,

Sir John Barleycorn.

Reading, June 12, 1826.

R. SNARE, PRINTER, MINSTER STREET, READING.

Election handbill for Palmer and Monck, 1826. They were in favour of the Beer Bill which would have benefited the consumer at the expense of the brewers. Palmer was defeated. The brewers were *not* in favour.

Tories turned their attention to Mr. Monck. At that time it was the custom for able-bodied men to apply at the workhouse and demand money, and by threats of violence they often obtained some. Mr. Monck was heavily rated, and a great part of his estate being within the borough he felt dissatisfied in having to contribute so largely towards the support of people who often expended what they obtained from the overseers in drink. He therefore, it was stated, hoped by adopting the following experiment to shame the able-bodied men from receiving parochial relief. Those he assisted of this class who were in the workhouse had the letters 'M.P.' made of cloth sewn on to their coat sleeves. In this case the letters were intended to make it known that these poor people were 'Monck's Poor.' I believe that the workhouse nuisance was by Mr. Monck's action considerably abated, if not entirely abolished. The opposing party, however, made the most of this business to the prejudice of his candidature, but their efforts were abortive, for Mr. Monck headed the poll. It was all along supposed that the contest would be a severe one, and so it proved, the result being: Monck, 418; Palmer, 399; Weyland, 394.

In 1827 it was resolved that Fyshe Palmer should be chaired. Public dinners were advertised at twenty of the principal inns for the accommodation of visitors. On Wednesday, April 18th, 1827, occurred one of the most extraordinary sights ever witnessed in Reading. The whole town was decorated with the Liberal flags and streamers, bells were ringing and bands playing from an early hour. Mr. Fyshe Palmer with Lady Madelina and some ladies arrived in a carriage and four, accompanied by a long following of carriages, horsemen, &c. Our Reading friends met them at the junction of the two London Roads, near the 'Granby' (a few years before the King's Road was formed), and the procession came down the London Road, London Street, &c. By this time all the windows were occupied by ladies, whose dresses and party-coloured ribbons gave life to the scene. Great interest was felt by the county families, and many of them were to be seen at the windows of most of the houses. I gave up my three balconies and drawing-room to Captain Montague and his family. As soon as the cavalcade turned from the London Road into London Street a flourish of trumpets was given which brought everybody to the windows, and the youngsters scampered out of the way shouting with excitement. First came a 'Herald' on a grey horse, dressed in orange costume, with a horseman on each side carrying banners with mottoes. These were followed by a long line of horsemen. Then a procession on foot with a military band, all being decorated with orange bows, flags, &c., &c. Then came Fyshe Palmer in his carriage and four, followed by a long line of carriages filled with gentlemen belonging to the county, in one of which was our old member Mr. J.B. Monck. I ought here to state that the carriage or triumphal car which Fyshe Palmer rode in was very beautiful, and was the work of the late Mr. Richard Sims, carver and gilder of London Street. Then came four trumpeters (lent by the Lord Mayor of London) who appeared in their rich city dress of velvet and velvet caps, the whole richly adorned with gold lace, followed by men carrying a very large green flag with the portrait of 'John Bull in his glory' on it, and lots of smaller ones with mottoes. Next came a Knight of the Forest, in superb brass armour with helmet and plumes, riding on a fine grey charger, accompanied by three mounted standard bearers. This was very attractive. The said Knight was followed by the cavalcade, headed by the Committee and accompanied by a full military band. Borne aloft was a large orange banner with the numbers of those who voted as determined by the Committee of the House of Commons:-

    PALMER   481
    SPENCE   458

A Knight of Malta, in a suit of steel armour, helmet with plume of feathers, mounted on a grey Arabian, came next, and then a long line of friends on foot with Union Jack, accompanied by a military band with white scarves; five gentlemen of the Body Guard mounted; then Mr. Fyshe Palmer, M.P., in a Roman triumphal car, drawn by six horses richly caparisoned, with postilions in orange jackets, decorated. In fact the whole thing was a miniature represenation of the Lord Mayor's procession, and it was a grand affair for a county town. I have no doubt that the procession exceeded a mile in length, and did not arrive at its destination, viz., the Crown Hotel, until nearly four o'clock.

A few minutes after the arrival Mr. Fyshe Palmer and Mr. Monck both appeared on the Crown balcony, and were received with loud cheering, which lasted some time. Mr. Monck, Mr. H. Marsh and others addressed the electors, after which they retired to be entertained with the best of all arguments after the fatigues of the day, viz., a good dinner. Our opponents did not appreciate the making of such a fuss over the 'Long Fyshe,' so on his procession day there was quite an exodus of the Blues; most of them had some relation or friend to visit in the country or in London, so there was no discordant element left in town, and I did not sit up to witness their return.

A section of the Blue party, composed principally of men of *deep thought,* persuaded themselves that the world would come to an end on the day in question. A tradesman in Broad Street was at the head of this movement, and he and his party emigrated to Tilehurst Common to witness the coming catastrophe, but what they saw or discovered was not divulged.

I have in my recollection an interesting story which was related in my presence in the year 1811, the 'Comet Year.' We had driven to Egham, where we left our horse and chaise, and next day travelled to London by the Englefield Green Coach. The driver was a Mr. Baverstock, who was held in high esteem I suppose, or he would not have been allowed to be so very familiar with the gentry. I should think that he has a traditional history at Egham. It was my first visit to London, and as regards Egham I have not been there since the year named. On our return we rode outside the coach, two other gentlemen from Egham being with us, sitting immediately behind the whip. On arriving at Hounslow Heath, a conversation occurred about the numerous highway robberies which had taken place there. My father, who about the year 1790 had resided at Staines, stated that in the latter part of the last century, a gentleman of the name of Fyshe Palmer, when on his way to London in a post chaise, was stopped on Hounslow Heath by a highwayman. The occupant opened the door at once, when a fellow on horseback thrust a pistol towards his face accompanied by the usual salutation. Mr. Palmer knocked the pistol on one side and instantly caught his assailant on the arm and pulled him off his horse into the chaise, at the same time shouting to the post boy to drive to Hounslow. If it was our late member into whose grasp the rascal had fallen (and I think it was), those who remember him as the 'Long Fyshe' will not be surprised to know that he captured his assailant, who was tried, convicted, and executed. It was also stated that the sum of thirty pounds from Government was at this time awarded on the conviction of a highwayman; it was called blood money. Mr. Palmer expended this amount on blankets, which were distributed to the poor of Wokingham.

In the beginning of the year 1831, the Reform Bill was before the House of Commons, and after long and exciting debates, in which O'Connell took part with the advocates of the measure, and Sir Charles Wetheral violently opposed it, the Bill was carried on the 22nd March by a majority of only one. With so small a majority, it was evidently of no use to go to the Lords; therefore Lord John Russell and Earl Grey appealed to the King, who dissolved Parliament on the 26th of April. Mr. Fyshe Palmer and Mr. Charles Russell were elected without opposition, both having supported the Bill. In June, Lord John Russell again introduced his Reform Bill with only trifling modification, and at the final division the Bill was carried by a majority of 109.

This decision was hailed with delight everywhere. In Reading a sort of spontaneous illumination occurred, and those who could do nothing better put candles in their windows, probably from fear of having the glass broken. The man employed by the Water Company at that time was Jerry Tibble, and upon festive occasions some of us subscribed for the purchase of gunpowder, and employed Jerry to fire off his cannon in the Forbury, but upon this occasion most of us lost our heads, and Jerry his, for he brought his cannon into London Street, near the Crown Hotel, where a political dinner was going on. Someone put a glass or two of wine out to Jerry, which had the desired effect, and our hero began ramming a cartridge into his cannon, but whether he had forgotten there was one in already I don't know. He was in the middle of the upper part of London Street, and seeing Captain Montague at a window he said 'Shall I fire, Sir?' 'Fire away, my man,' said the Captain, and Jerry Tibble did fire, bursting his cannon and destroying all the glass in the windows as far down as Church Street. The scene that followed was laughable. The houses were quickly emptied of their inmates, for the people said there was an earthquake. Jerry was blown towards Silver Street, but was not much hurt. His cannon had disappeared, and he was so mobbed by people who had suffered by the explosion that he could not get away until he was shorn of some garments. In the end, as Captain Montague had said 'Fire away, my man,' Jerry stuck to him, and the Captain paid £26 odd. Luckily there was no plate-glass included, and no one to sympathise with the Captain excepting a man interested in the glass trade, who witnessed this mad affair.

The Government, after a most gallant struggle, obtained the Royal assent to the Bill on the 7th June, 1832. The news was received in Reading with demonstrations of joy, and illuminations were hastily arranged by some people, but it was determined that a day should be appointed for a general holiday, and that a dinner should be given to the poor and all those who chose to partake of it. This arrangement was carried out in a magnificent manner on Wednesday, the 18th July, 1832. Tables were erected on both sides of London Street, each table capable of seating 60 persons. My people cooked the dinner for the table opposite my house and I had the honour of carving. It was pretty much the same in every instance, each householder feeling bound to contribute what assistance they could. The tables were continued through Duke Street, King Street, Market Place, Friar, West and Broad Streets. All the tables were decorated with evergreens, which had a pleasing effect. Guns were fired, bells rung and bands played. 7,000 persons sat down to dinner, and all enjoyed themselves to their heart's content. Mr. Monck was the principal chairman, and Dr. Valpy offered up a fervent prayer before the repast began. A great many people came into the town from the country, and seemed most delighted; it was a glorious sight to see so many people happy. All passed off well, and taking into consideration the difficulty of seating and providing a dinner for 7,000 persons upwards, it is a marvel that no discordant element arose to mar the success of the arrangements.

On the 13th of December 1834, we had to mourn the loss of our highly esteemed neighbour, John Berkeley Monck, of Coley Park. Mr. Monck had served us faithfully in Parliament for a long time, and only retired in 1830 after passing the Beer Bill. I remember that there was some difference of opinion in the Liberal ranks as to Mr. Monck's vote on this question, but experience proved that he was right, and it was not long before the advocates of temperance appealed to Parliament in order to have the Act modified in the sense in which Mr. Monck voted.

The loss of so good a man was felt by all parties, and this was exemplified at the funeral, when some four or five hundred of the electors, including the Freemasons, assembled at Coley Avenue and accompanied the cortège, forming four abreast, to the Church of St. Mary's. All the shops in Castle Street were closed, with their blinds down, and I was informed that a great many places of business in other parts of the town were likewise closed. A meeting was subsequently convened in the Council Chamber and an address of condolence agreed to be presented to Mrs. Monck and family; all political parties concurring.

The Lecture given by Mr. Brain and the quotations from Mr. Justice Talfourd's works, as reported in the *Observer,* are very interesting, and evoke in my memory long-forgotten events. With reference to Mr. Justice Talfourd's age and place of birth, his sister, who is living in our midst, would settle those points in a moment. My sister, Miss. E. Silver, of Ouseleaze, Wargrave, was born on the 13th December, 1794, and the late Edward Vines informed me that he had dined with her and a party of friends at Wargrave, when a conversation occurred in reference to a coming election. Fyshe Palmer was one of the guests, and Talfourd's name and age having been referred to, it was stated that my sister was about two months his senior.

But the greatest puzzle to me is the statement that Talfourd 'received his education under Dr. Valpy,' and yet that he was only 18 months with him. I have already stated what I knew of the masters - Foley, Jameson and Bath - and also that I knew many of the pupils. In Talfourd's addresses both at Reading and Abingdon at the time of his election to the Bench, his education at Dr. Valpy's is alluded to. I cannot conceive that this statement as to time can be correct, for I was constantly seeing him either on his way to or from the school, usually by the entrance in Vastern Lane.

I remember when very young being taken to Broad Street Chapel, and hearing a gentleman, who I think must have been Mr. Douglas, preach, probably his first sermon; all I recollect of him at that time was an awkward way he had of drawing himself up and then leaning over his pulpit. On leaving the chapel my father, seeing Talfourd, said to me: 'You should try and be as clever as he, for when he arrives at his home in all probability he will write down the sermon he has heard this morning.'

I have an impression that Talfourd's first brief was given him by Mr. Vines, senr., in a case of some importance tried at our assizes in which

Dr. Hooper was plaintiff (I believe), and the judge in summing up complimented the young barrister, but I have no record of this.

When Mr. Talfourd became a candidate for the representation of his 'native town,' I attended most of the meetings, as also the preliminary ones held at Mr. Vines' office. On his committee I met there the late Mr. Gilchrist, a Unitarian minister, who did good service in publicly addressing the electors from the windows of one of the houses in the Market Place.

Allusion has been made to Mr. Talfourd's speech at the time of the Peterloo affair. I may remind our friends that Sir. F. Burdett also made a speech upon the same untoward event, for which he was tried and sentenced I think, to a year's imprisonment and a fine of one thousand pounds; this sum the public began to subscribe, but Sir. F. Burdett stopped the movement. So popular was he, however, that tobacco and snuff boxes were cast in metal, and on the lids were profiles of him with this inscription: 'Westminster's Pride and England's Hope.'

When the New Hall in London Street was erected some of us Liberals agreed to call the place the Mechanics' Institution, and lectures, sermons, balls, &c., were held there, but the mechanics made no sign. Here Talfourd, Dickens, Vincent and others used to give lectures. I, amongst many others, took shares in this venture; those I have lie at the bottom of my iron chest waiting for the first dividend!

I am not certain of having alluded to the following anecdote, showing the ready wit of Mr. Talfourd in early days. As a matter of local history there was at the beginning of this century a Literary Institution (a Mr. Kemp living in the Forbury being the curator), of which Society I am inclined to think I am the only surviving member. In its decline the Philosophical Institution was established. The members of both these, some 40 or more years since, dined together at the Upper Ship, Sergeant Talfourd being there with Dr. Mitford, Robert Harris, the banker, Peter Green, the agriculturist, Mr. Kitcat, formerly a Unitarian Minister, Messrs. George Cooper, Morris, Vines and some fifty others. After the loyal toasts the Chairman proposed the toast of the authoress of 'Our Village.' Dr. Mitford, who sat at the head of the table where I was, seemed to have enjoyed his dinner, and on rising to respond in rather a hurry, was troubled with shortness of breath, he being a stout man. When he began to speak a troublesome cough suggested a glass of wine, which he simply threw down his throat, as an antidote. This, instead of allaying the irritation, brought matters to a crisis. His attempts to speak were so ridiculous that some of the company broke out into a loud laugh, which so aggravated the Doctor that he was red in the face with rage. As soon as he could speak he called out 'What the devil are you laughing at?' Then he said 'Talfourd, you must finish for me.' Mr. Talfourd rose to alleviate the sufferings of the poor man, but he could not begin until he had indulged in another laugh, which the company joined in. The learned gentleman apologised for his friend's break down, and then made a charming address, eulogising Miss Mitford as an honour to her sex, &c., &c., and finishing by proposing the health of the 'Author of the Authoress.' The Doctor then spoke fairly well, and with thanks to the Chairman, we separated.

The commencement of the year 1850 was one of difficulty for magistrates, and indeed for all whose duty it was to see that the peace was not broken. Messrs. Cobden and Bright had been addressing the people on the question of Free Trade, and very recently had invaded our county, so that not only landlords but farmers became alarmed. This led to a meeting of the agriculturists; and the adoption of a requisition signed by 1,300 people, which was presented to the High Sheriff, who very soon held a public meeting at our Town Hall for the purpose of discussing their grievances, and to organise resistance. The High Sheriff occupied the chair, and was supported by Mr. Robert Palmer, M.P., Mr. Job Lowsley (who at this period frequently published letters on agriculture in our local papers), Earl Radnor, the Marquis of Downshire, Mr. Mount and others. It was the noisiest meeting I ever attended, but having gone to it early I was near the reporters, and therefore probably heard more of the speeches than those in the body of the Hall. It seemed at one time that no one would attempt a speech, and it was not until the High Sheriff had appealed to the meeting several times to keep order that the new Member for Reading, Mr. Stanford, rose to address the meeting. This gentleman, who, it was alleged, became our M.P. by a fluke, had announced his determination to marry a Reading lady, and this had produced an unusual flutter, and an accelerated sale of ribbons and dresses of the Cambridge tint. As soon as the honourable gentleman began to speak at the meeting he was assailed with good-humoured questions of 'How's your missus?' 'How's your wife?' 'When is she coming home?' &c. As may be supposed there was a general laugh - not a party one - for no one probably but his immediate friends knew which side he would take; but when he spoke disparagingly of Bright and Cobden, I could not catch another word for the noise produced by the conflicting parties at the other end of the room. It was so great that it prevented even the reporters from hearing. Major Court spoke on the other side; but what he said could not be heard. Lord Downshire said if the tumult continued he would head the farmers and clear the hall. This threat produced one of the most excited scenes I ever witnessed, for there was a general fight, hats and sticks flying in all directions. The farmers combined and eventually drove the enemy before them into Friar Street. Here they assisted the police, who were too few to withstand the roughs, they having overpowered them both inside and outside the hall. When order had been restored, Mr. Weedon, in an energetic and argumentative speech upon the subject before the meeting, severely condemned the utterances of the Marquis of Downshire for threatening to clear the hall of those who differed from him. At the break-up of the meeting the farmers had to defend themselves from the fury of the mob and to seek protection in shops or inns. In the Market Place the Mayor, in trying to protect two friends, was himself assailed, but he fought his way and knocked one of his assailants off his legs. Some time subsequent to this I myself had occasion for a lot of specials, and I swore in all the roughs who were usually troublesome, and decorated them with a white band on the hat and arm, of which they seemed proud, and the peace was not broken.

—12—

Work in Local Government

W.S. Darter, constable for St. Giles' parish and councillor for the borough - a Corporation dinner - farewell.

It may be a matter of astonishment for my fellow-townsmen to know that, 70 years ago, we had but one watchman for the whole of St. Giles' parish and no police; and yet this man, whose name was Norcroft, seemed never to get into trouble, but when necessary would call on a bystander to aid and assist in the King's name, and if his appeal was not responded to the delinquent was heavily fined. I remember well Norcroft's features and the sound of his voice 'Past two o'clock and a cloudy mornin', &c.

We had no police, but a head constable was chosen from the ratepayers on the election of Mayor, and he selected a number of others to serve under him, the names being submitted to the Chief Magistrate before being sworn.

In the 1830s riots were constantly occurring at St. Giles' workhouse in Horn Street, when able-bodied men demanded money with threats of violence. During this period I became Constable, and had a number of assistants, I think twelve. Mr. Bunce, the upholsterer, living on the premises now Mr. Long's, in London Street, was Overseer, and he applied to me for protection, as upon a late occasion the roughs followed him to his place of business and hammered away at his shutters so that his family became alarmed for their safety. I had made myself aquainted with the characters of these men, and on one occasion, after they had taken money, I followed them and discovered that the money so obtained was spent gambling at a public house in Silver Street. An arrangement was made on a pay night to have the constables at a house very near the workhouse, and at the moment when these fellows were knocking away at the gates we came upon them unobserved and

Darter's house in London Street, formerly no. 26 but now 54. The three balconied drawing room windows from which Captain Montague watched the grand procession in 1827 can still be seen.

captured all but one. I returned with Mr. Bunce to his house in London Street about half-past ten, and seeing a tall man on the other side increasing his speed I ran towards him, and as he bolted I came up with him near the Savings' Bank, tripped him up, and calling on a man who was passing to aid and assist 'in the King's name,' I secured him. Thus ended these unseemly proceedings in St. Giles' parish, and I believe that nothing of the kind ever occurred again.

Almost all our Municipal elections were at this time fought upon political grounds, but personally I took no active part in local matters until the year 1847, when I had an unexpected 'honour thrust upon me.' It occurred in this way. The late Alderman Lewis having died, Mr. John Yard Willats, senr., was elected to succeed him. This created a vacancy in Church Ward, and a gentleman living in Portland Place issued a handbill announcing himself as a candidate. Next day to my astonishment I saw a printed paper in a shop window with my signature attached, stating that as a native of the town and connected with its trade (in which I felt deep interest), I had been invited by a numerous body of electors to offer my services, &c. I gave no authority for this, for up to the moment of my seeing this handbill I had not the most remote idea of accepting the suggested honour. Having obtained a copy of the said handbill I took it in my perplexity to my neighbour Lovejoy; he has been a good deal connected with the press, and I asked his advice as to the propriety of my repudiating the whole thing. He tried to put on a serious look, but by his manner I suspected that he knew something about it, for he said 'If I were you I would let it go, and take no notice of it.' I soon found that he whose counsel I sought had, with the assistance and concurrence of Mr. Cowderoy, written and issued the said handbill. The effect of this was that the gentleman before referred to retired from the field, and left me to walk over the course.

The second municipal contest in which I was concerned occurred only three weeks after my unopposed election. A few days prior to these events, and fearing a contest, my friends had taken a Committee-room at an Inn which belonged to an opposing brewer. On the morning in question, at an early hour, my opponents took forcible possession of this room and also another in Crown Street, but we were offered one at the Crown Hotel which we engaged; we were, however, placed between two fires, and so provoked were my opponents, who, by the bye, had got wind of this movement of the Radical section of our party late on Saturday night, that they prepared some questionable literature, both in prose and verse, in which I was assailed for offences of which I was innocent, and, on the other side, had virtues attributed to me which I never possessed.

My friend, Mr. Cowderoy, who was kind enough to act as Chairman of my Committee, informed me that our opponents had determined to give a luncheon to those supporters who chose to partake of it, and, amongst other things, had provided a round of beef so that the working men need not go home to dinner after having voted. What shall *we* do? asked my Chairman. I felt in a difficulty, for my party had on their flags 'No bribery, no treating, purity of election, &c.' I confess that my moral courage gave way, and I, too, ordered luncheon, with a *sotto voce* hint that I would fight them with their own weapons; this we did, and beat our opponents by two to one. I don't suggest that beef or beer had anything to do with the result.

The first Corporation dinner that I attended was held at the Bear Inn (at that time one of the old posting establishments). I had been informed that the junior member of the Council would have the honour of taking the vice-chair, with the distinguished name of 'Boots at the Bear.' How this silly custom originated I have no idea, but with the aid of the Schoolmaster our habits are changed for the better in reference to excess drinking at public dinners. At the time I refer to, now forty years since, it was the custom for gentlemen to take wine with each other at these entertainments, and those sitting at a distance would send the waiter to say that Mr. So-and-so would be happy to take wine with you. On reflection it occurred to me that my new office was one of difficulty, for how could I avoid taking wine with those who challenged me ? Upon this occasion, as anticipated, I had a good deal more attention paid to me than I desired, for I was constantly bowing, and sipping, and thought that these jovial friends expected to see me under the table. I, however, responded to their challenge without any visible effect being produced. On my right sat Mr. George Cooper, and on my left Mr. Brown, father of the present gentleman of that name, living in Castle Street. The dinner was nearly over when Mr. Cooper challenged his opposite friend Brown to take wine with him, and with much pleasure responded Mr. Brown. Mr. Cooper, unobserved by me, passed my decanter to his friend, who bowed and essayed to drink, but holding in his mouth what he had taken for wine he suddenly dropped it into his plate. 'Why, Cooper, what have you given me?' said Mr. Brown. Mr. Cooper broke out into one of his hearty laughs, which drew the attention of the whole company to us. No one but himself and Mr. Brown knew the cause of this sudden merriment. Mr. Cooper rose and said 'Mr. Mayor, I have to accuse our Vice-Chairman of a breach of good manners, for he has been drinking toast and water all the evening, and I have only just now found him out.' This caused a general demand for the removal of the offending decanter, which was speedily obeyed. I, however, had the advantage of most of the gentlemen present, for I was prepared to begin to spend the evening and enjoy it.

Previous to the dinner I had an idea that unless I was particularly careful, my 'evening's amusement would not bear the morning's reflection,' and I should feel none the better for a public feast. On the morning of the dinner, it occurred to me that toast and water would suit me better than wine; I, therefore, called at the Bear Hotel and asked for the head waiter, and to him I expressed my desire to have a decanter of the former prepared as nearly as possible the colour of sherry, and they could (if they liked) charge for it as wine, which would compensate them for their trouble, but they must take care to place it before my seat. This order was literally obeyed, to my great comfort.

Captain Hodges, one of our Aldermen and an old Waterloo Officer, seemed to enjoy himself remarkably well, and was rather more attentive to me in the way of taking wine than I cared for. He frequently called on me to pass the decanters, to the risk of losing my own. He eventually became very merry, and some one sang a song, and then the Alderman referred to was requested to use his musical powers. 'I will do my best, Mr. Mayor,' replied the captain, 'but I don't think you will ask me again.' Off went our friend: 'At the Seige of Bellile, I was there all the while, I was there all the while at the Seige of Bellile.' This was the song, and he kept on like a piece of machinery, and would not yield to a friendly shaking of those who sat near him, till at last the company gradually dispersed, including the Vice-Chairman, who with a few friends retired to have a rubber and finish the night with 'devilled Turkey' and a glass of grog. At what time Alderman Hodges finished the 'Seige of Bellile' is at present unknown.

123

In bringing these recollections to a close, I hope not to have given offence to any of those who are descended from the people to whom I have alluded. I also venture to hope that another day what I have written may arouse and keep alive in the minds of younger men an increased interest in their native town. Possibly the same subject may be taken up by younger men, whose power of description will be less homely than those of one who made his appearance in Reading two years before 'Nelson fell.' If I have done wrong in publishing these reminiscences, the greater culprits are some half-dozen friends, who now and again heard me speak of something which occurred in my early years. Therefore I hope that any pugnacious reader will vent his anger on them and let your correspondent escape.

OCTOGENARIAN.

October 10th, 1887.

Index